Turbulent
Change

Turbulent Change

Change

Every Working Person's
Survival Guide

Peter R. Garber

DAVIES-BLACK PUBLISHING
PALO ALTO, CALIFORNIA

Published by Davies-Black Publishing, an imprint of Consulting Psychologists Press, Inc., 3803 East Bayshore Road, Palo Alto, CA 94303; 800-624-1765.

Special discounts on bulk quantities of Davies-Black books are available to corporations, professional associations, and other organizations. For details, contact the Director of Book Sales at Davies-Black Publishing, an imprint of Consulting Psychologists Press, Inc., 3803 East Bayshore Road, Palo Alto, CA 94303; 650-691-9123; Fax 650-623-9271.

Visit the Davies-Black Publishing web site at www.cpp-db.com

Cover illustration by Ed Taber

03 02 01 00 99   10 9 8 7 6 5 4 3 2 1
Printed in the United States of America

Library of Congress Cataloging-in-Publication Data

Garber, Peter R.
  Turbulent change : every working person's survival guide / Peter R. Garber
  p.   cm.
  Includes index.
  ISBN 0-89106-135-5 (pbk.)
  1. Organizational change. 2. Career changes. I. Title.
HD58.8.G367 1999   99-33219
658.4—dc21   CIP

FIRST EDITION
First printing 1999

With love to my family

for all the many changes we go through together

CONTENTS

―――

Preface

Do you like change? Most people look forward to change with the same enthusiasm they have toward having a root canal done at the dentist. Change just isn't something that most people welcome into their lives. But change is constantly happening to us at work and in our personal lives. Like it or not, we have to put up with it. The better you can learn to navigate your way through change, the more effective you'll become in dealing with it. This book explores people's feelings, attitudes, and ideas about change. It is full of exercises, stories, and questionnaires to help you understand change and deal with it intelligently in the future.

Regardless of how you may feel about it, change is here to stay. "The only constant around here is change" is an adage that will become even truer as time goes on. You may not be able to do anything about the changes occurring in your organization, but you can do something about how you react to them. Although this may seem like a small step, it's actually a giant leap toward changing your attitude about change and the impact it can have on your future.

Today's organizations are changing at a phenomenal pace. Nothing happens in a vacuum; everything has ripple effects. These changes can be caused by any number of events: new leadership, new acquisitions, new technology, market shifts, world events, politics, and more. No sooner does one change end than another begins. These changes come in a variety of forms and may be called by many different names such as downsizing, rightsizing, reengineering, realignment, or streamlining. No matter what the change is called, the result remains the same. People's lives are affected one way or another. Sometimes these changes may be viewed as positive. Change doesn't always have to mean trouble. It can bring new ways of doing business that make life easier and better for everyone. But change can also cause people to experience great anxiety and frustration as the familiar and comfortable are replaced by something very unfamiliar, even frightening.

In our information age, the hectic pace creates even more rapid changes than in the past. Today's new communication tools are making it possible to share information with others in just seconds rather than days, weeks, or longer. Personal computers, faxes, voice mail systems, pagers, satellite dishes, electronic mail, answering machines, the Internet and Intranets, and other innovations have completely changed the way we do business and communicate with one another. No matter how remote a location or part of the organization, it can be put online and kept up-to-date on everything that's happening. And all of this is accelerating the rate of change and reorganization every day.

No matter how you may be personally affected, you can learn to cope better with the changes occurring in your organization and learn to welcome change, not just survive it. When change knocks, you need to answer the door and invite it into your life. This book can help you become part of the welcoming committee when change comes to visit your organization—as it has a habit of frequently doing, almost always without invitation!

As a human resource professional and specialist in organizational change, I've been helping people on all levels of the organization learn to deal with change for nearly two decades. I have dealt with change in a variety of business settings, and it is from these experiences that I've developed the ideas presented in this book. One thing seems clear to me: The people who have been most successful in their careers are often those who have been the most receptive to change. These success stories include those who seem to perceive change not as a threat but as an opportunity. They have learned to anticipate it—even look forward to its arrival. It is my sincerest hope that this book will help you begin to think about change in a similar manner.

About the Author

Peter R. Garber is Manager of Teamwork Development for PPG Industries, Inc., in Pittsburgh, Pennsylvania. Since joining the company in 1980, he has held a variety of human resource positions at a number of the company's manufacturing facilities in addition to his present assignment at its corporate offices in Pittsburgh. In his current role, he provides consultative services, training, seminars, and guidance on a wide range of management topics to associates at all levels of the organization.

Garber is the author of a number of business-related books including *Coaching Self-Directed Workteams, 30 Easy-to-Use Reengineering Activities, 25 SkillBuilding Activities for Supervisors and Managers, Diversity Explorations. Team Skillbuilders, 25 Customer Service Icebreakers and Activities, 101 Ways to Build a Better Relationship with the Customer,* and *25 Sales Strategies & Training Activities,* and he is coauthor of the popular *101 Stupid Things Supervisors Do to Sabotage Success.* He has also published numerous articles and teaching tools on human resource and business subjects.

Garber received his bachelor's degree in English from the University of Pittsburgh and his master's degree in guidance and personnel from St. Bonaventure University. He is married and has two daughters.

Chapter 1

Hearing the News

Things are going to change. It is not within your power to do much about that fact. But how you *react* to change is certainly within your control. Getting in control of yourself during these stressful times is an important first step.

Imagine that an organizational change has just been announced. What should you do? Panic would only make things worse. This is a time you need to think more clearly than ever before. What you do during the earliest stages of organizational change may be the most critical to your success in the new scheme of things to come.

First of all, get over it! Take a deep breath, count to ten, close your door—and kick your wastepaper basket across your office if you must. In short, do whatever you must to find an appropriate outlet to vent the emotions and frustrations you may be experiencing as a result of the announcement.

Change is not only inevitable but necessary. Imagine where we'd be if nothing ever changed. Even so, feeling good about change is not always easy. Change forces us to leave behind skills we have taken a lot of trouble to master. It forces us out of our comfort zone into the world of the unknown. These can be scary first steps—much like walking out on thin ice on a frozen lake not knowing if you'll make it to shore before it cracks and sends you falling into the waters below.

But change isn't the worst thing that can happen to you. What if nothing ever changed? It might be like the comedy movie *Groundhog Day*. In that movie Bill Murray's character was forced to relive the same day over and over again. For much of the movie he tried to move on in his life but nothing changed. Instead he found himself stuck in Punxsutawney, Pennsylvania, celebrating Groundhog Day day after day. Although everything remaining the same might sound appealing, even comforting, it would quickly get old. Like Bill Murray, you might soon be trying to find ways to make something—anything—change!

How you adapt to change may be one of the most important skills you can learn to ensure a successful future. The ability to adapt and learn new skills quickly can make the difference between those who thrive during organizational change as opposed to merely surviving (or not even surviving at all). Think of the following story as a sort of test. How will *you* react to the future organizational changes you'll experience? Imagine what you might do if faced with a similar set of circumstances. The story illustrates the importance of developing the key skills you'll need to adapt to organizational change during these turbulent times. The good news is that not only can these skills be learned but they can be mastered by anyone on any level of the organization. This book is designed to teach you these critical skills as well as challenge any unproductive perceptions you may have about dealing with change. The main character in this story, James Brewer, has not yet learned many of these skills—as is painfully evident by his behavior and actions.

Another Organizational Change

Just a few short months ago, the view from James Brewer's office window at the Distribution Center never looked so good. As manager of the center, he and his team had met or exceeded every one of the company's goals for on-time delivery and inventory management. Since the completion of an innovative bar-coding project (James' brainchild), they could now track a shipment with such accuracy that it was even scary at times. "I hope the company never decides to bar-code *me* and trace my every move!" he joked to his friends and coworkers at the Distribution Center.

The project involved installing a software program that creates and prints a bar-code label for each piece of inventory. The bar-coded information includes a complete profile on the product as well as all the shipping information that's needed to trace a delivery once it leaves the center. Another valuable feature of this new process is that once the product arrives, customers simply have to scan the bar code using a special "reader device" to record that it arrived and to enter it into their inventory control system. This information can then be transmitted between the Distribution Center and the customer to allow reorders to be completed automatically by the new computerized inventory system. Although this innovation represented a major change in the way things were done at the Distribution Center, everyone was getting used to this new system as they realized how much easier it was making their jobs. James was beginning to feel good about these changes, too, and was finally getting control of his work life and personal life.

That feeling abruptly changed one day when he received an interoffice memo about a major organizational change. Over the years, James had seen changes come and go and he had survived them all. These changes went by many different names such as realignment, restructuring, reorganization, and most recently reengineering. Whatever they were called, they all amounted to the same thing: change. (He often wondered why these changes always seemed to begin with the letters "re.") He figured he'd do what he'd always done in the past to weather the storm by keeping a low profile for a while. He'd make it look like he was going along with the program and simply ride it out until the wave passed like all of its predecessors. This one, however, concerned him more than the others. This time the memo seemed to convey a sense of foreboding. All he was told was that he'd learn more about these impending changes in the near future and that for now no new initiatives were to be begun until these announcements were made. "At least there's still a future," he tried to reassure himself. That evening he went home in a terrible mood, something he hadn't done in a long time.

James didn't mean to take his work problems home with him. It wasn't his family's fault that he was feeling so anxious about the impending changes. It was just the uncertainty of not knowing what was going to happen next and how he was going to be affected. That's what seemed to worry him most. In the past, he had always felt sure that the changes were going to hit some other department or someone else. This one sounded like it was going to strike a little closer to home.

"Why do they have to keep changing everything all the time?" he complained to his wife that evening at dinner.

"You need to take it easy, James," his wife advised him as they cleared the dishes from the table. "Don't go getting yourself all upset about things you don't yet understand. You'll just make things worse with this attitude."

"What do you mean? I'm not the one who wants to change everything—especially now that things are finally beginning to run smoothly," James replied.

"No, that's true. But the way you react to the changes is within your control. You've always survived the changes in the past. Everything will turn out just fine. Don't worry," she counseled her husband.

Unfortunately, James did not follow his wife's advice. He went back to work with an even worse attitude about accepting future changes. Everything was already going just fine, he insisted, and he kept saying to anyone who would listen: "If it ain't broke, why fix it?"

By the time the reorganization was finally announced, James had convinced himself and everyone else in the center that it was going to be a horror show. In reality, the changes had the potential of giving him greater opportunities to move the concepts of automated distribution systems forward in the organization. Unfortunately, he was so focused on the negative aspects of the changes that he couldn't see these benefits.

Instead of taking advantage of the opportunities that the changes might have brought, James continued to resist them and clung desperately to the past. Rather than share his extensive knowledge of the inventory and distribution system in the new organization, he kept to himself and hoped the new organization would just go away. He criticized every aspect of the changes and only did the absolute minimum in support of the change.

But the change was here to stay. Instead of growing with the new organization, James ended up in a less important role. He never really seemed to understand that it was his attitude about the changes, more than anything else, that caused the problems for him.

Don't Burn Your Bridges

Change can create a very emotional time. Don't let your emotions get the best of you during these critical moments. You may say or do things you may regret later on. No matter how upset you may be today, you'll still need a job tomorrow.

This is not to suggest that you should hide all your feelings. You should express your concerns and try to find out how legitimate they really are. But you need to do it in an appropriate, professional, nondestructive manner. Listen carefully to the reasons why these changes were made. Find out what's expected of everyone to support these new initiatives. This can be particularly important in the early stages of the change process. Remember that ultimately you will be judged on how well you supported the change, not how upset you were. Thus it's important to channel your energy in the right direction. This was something James Brewer failed to do, and it turned out to be a big mistake. Instead of being seen by others in the organization as a key contributor to making the changes work, he was viewed as an anchor—something that has to be dragged along and slows down progress.

A bridge is something that allows you to proceed over an obstacle that could cause you serious delay or even halt your progress. As we travel by car or train, bridges allow us to move across water, valleys, or difficult terrain. We come to bridges in our careers, as well, and we can choose to cross or not. These bridges may not be made of wood, stone, or steel, but they do help us get where we're headed. Instead of building bridges to help you get where you want to go in the future, an attitude like James Brewer's only burns them down.

Think of organizational change as another bridge you come to in your career. How can this bridge lead to future roads? How can you fortify these bridges of change to let you cross safely? Or, conversely, how might you burn down these bridges and thus block your progress? Looking at it this way, burning down these bridges to the future is not something anyone would consciously want to do. Why, then, do so many people do it?

Maybe it's because change often disguises itself as an obstacle rather than a bridge. By resisting change we might think we're removing a barrier in our way when in fact we are burning down an important bridge. James Brewer saw the next organizational change as a barrier to accomplishing his goal of improving the efficiency of his company's distribution system. So he destroyed this bridge—and consequently blocked his own career progress. Someone else crossed the bridge instead, leaving James on the other side of change wondering why he wasn't there. When changes are made, organizations will be *assessing* the damage it may have caused in terms of how people are reacting. You don't really want to get on their casualty list of victims—the list of those who aren't going to survive much less thrive during the forthcoming changes. The following sections offer some dos and don'ts to help you avoid burning your bridges during organizational change.

Don't Self-Destruct

As much as you'd love to see the changes go away and everything be like it used to, there's not much chance it will happen. You're bound to experience some strong emotions. Feeling upset and anxious about a significant change in your life, whether at work or at home, is a perfectly natural reaction. The point is that you shouldn't let these feelings cause you to become self-destructive. Venting your emotions during times of change in an appropriate and professional manner is one thing. Taking these emotions so far that you actually do harm to your reputation, career, and relationships is something else entirely. Every change brings with it a feeling of loss. In this sense, experiencing change is like mourning the loss of someone or something important to you. Understand that you will go through these emotions and that you need to find a way to continue with your life despite this loss. Time can be your biggest ally in making these difficult life adjustments. Just don't let your emotions cause you to do or say anything you may regret later on.

Don't Cry over Spilled Milk

It's amazing how quickly we forget some of the most valuable lessons from our childhood when it comes to organizational change—lessons like the old proverb "Don't cry over spilled milk." Maybe the best thing to do when you first hear that something is about to change in your organization is to pick up the phone and ask your mother if she's still mad about that lamp you broke so many years ago. You'll find that what was once a very upsetting experience is now just a memory. She probably remembers what both of you learned from the experience—and, despite all the tears, how insignificant it was in the larger scope of things. What does this tell you about your present reaction to changes occurring in your organization today?

Watch What You Say

Remember that cubicles have ears. This doesn't mean Big Brother is watching and listening to everything you say. And it doesn't mean your phone is tapped or there are hidden microphones all over the building. What it means is there are very few secrets in the workplace. People just hear things in the normal course of their workday. If you work in a cubicle, as more and more people do today, there is little that goes on in your life that your office neighbors don't know about. As the cartoon character Dilbert is constantly discovering, work life in a cubicle does create interpersonal challenges! How realistic do you think the following dialogue would be in a typical organization experiencing major changes?

"I hear Jerry is really upset about the reorganization. I understand he's looking for another job."

"Is that right? How do you know?"

"I heard him on the phone yesterday. He has an interview in Chicago on Tuesday with some big company."

"Oh, yeah? I have to go wish him luck."

"No, don't. He doesn't want anyone to know!"

"Okay, I won't say anything to him. Hmmm. I wonder who'll get his job when he leaves?"

Chances are this conversation could take place in virtually any workplace. Maybe you've even taken part in a similar conversation. (By the way, who do you think is going to get Jerry's job when he leaves?)

Don't Begin Your Own Silent Protest

Protests may be effective during times of social turmoil, but they have no place in the business world today, no matter how subtle they may be. A silent protest can be conducted in many different ways. It may be a refusal to acknowledge that a certain change has been initiated—continuing to use old terminology that was changed as part of the reorganization, for example, or refusing to use new technology or new procedures instituted at significant expense.

Becoming a martyr for the rest of the organization may bear a greater price than you really want to pay. Although such protest might gain some early support from coworkers who feel they've been treated unfairly, ultimately you will lose the support of the majority of others who did adapt to the changes in the organization. They may begin to resent the fact that they had to go along with the change and you didn't. Or they may begin to see you as an obstacle to progress rather than a defender of their past. "Either help us or get out of the way" best summarizes how others will begin to feel about those who persist in resisting change.

And don't feed the rumor mill with reports detailing how upset you are about the changes. Although this may feel good in the short term, it could come back to haunt you later in your career. One thing you never want to do is send an angry letter to the higher-ups in your organization complaining about how unfairly you've been treated as a result of new changes. A letter like that could very well end up in your permanent personnel file like a ticking time bomb ready to explode at a later date in your career. The lesson here is simple: If you're going to make a fool of yourself, don't create a permanent record of it for future generations of bosses.

Don't Say Anything You'll Regret

Once you've said it, you can never really take it back. Even the sincerest apology can't totally undo what has already been stated. "Loose lips sink ships" is as true when it comes to organizational change as it is in naval security. Before you explode in frustration or anger, make sure your brain has had a chance to consider the long-term implications of what you're about to say. Organizations seem to have incredibly long memories for such things. Similarly, don't immediately take a polarized position or make claims that you may not want to fulfill. Insisting that "I'm never going to go along with that change" may only demonstrate just how weak your convictions are if ultimately you're forced to go along. As the changes become inevitable, such statements only put you in a lose-lose position. Don't pick battles you have no way of winning. And don't say things you can never live up to during times of change.

Maintain Your Self-Esteem

You are the same person you were before the change was announced. If you felt good about yourself before, don't let the new changes affect your self-perceptions. Why should they? There are countless reasons why people are repositioned during organizational change—many of which have nothing to do with their competence or performance. Others quickly pick up on how you're feeling about yourself. If you think of yourself as someone who should be pitied, that's the way people will begin to treat you. But if you're seen as having a strong character, even when things are not going your way, you'll be treated in a different manner. The experience can become one of enhancing your self-esteem and consequently the image you project throughout the organization. If the thought of becoming more respected in the organization as a result of being passed over for a promotion seems a little far-fetched, think of it like this: There is nothing else you can do about it that wouldn't be self-destructive. Regardless of how you feel, you'll find it more beneficial to act like a winner, not a whiner, in the new organization. Besides, who would *you* rather have in the next cubicle?

Strengthen Your Working Relationships

Your relationships with others in the organization become even more important during times of change. Think of maintaining your working relationships with others in the organization as strengthening the bridges that help reach your ultimate goals in the future. Many of these relationship bridges take a long time to develop. Maintaining them is like doing bridge repair. The best time to do the repair is *before* the bridge falls down. Although changes in the organization will stress these relationships, it's up to you to keep them intact. Sometimes you may not come to a bridge for a long time, so it's easy to forget just how important a connection it is. Be sure to maintain good bridge repair—particularly during times of organizational change.

Building these stronger relationships is like pouring cement into bridge supports or abutments. When crossing a long expansion bridge over water, doesn't it always make you feel better to see those huge supportive structures underneath ensuring your safety? Engineers design a bridge to accommodate the *maximum* stress it will experience, not merely the minimum or even the average. To do otherwise would lead to certain disaster. The question to ask yourself is this: Are my working relationships strong enough to bear the maximum stress they may experience during times of organizational change? Or will they hold together only when it's business as usual?

Tolls and Trolls

There are costs associated with nearly every change you face in life. These costs can be experienced in many different ways. Some costs are relatively low and easily paid, while others come at a much higher price. Exercises 1 and 2 ask you to identify some of the costs you have encountered in your experiences with change.

CAREER TOLLS

Many bridges we cross in life require us to pay a toll for their use. On the highway the price may vary from a few cents to a few dollars per car. Everyone who uses the bridge must pay this fee. No one gets across for free. When we come to bridges in our careers, there's often a toll we must pay as well. No one gets across these career bridges without at least some cost or sacrifice. But these costs are different than simply throwing a few coins in a basket to lift a barrier. If only crossing our career bridges were that simple! These costs are usually more emotional than financial. They represent many of the fears, frustrations, and anxieties we experience on our career journeys. Take a few moments and think about what some of these tolls have been as you crossed bridges from one change to the next in your career. What are the main career tolls you have had to pay?

....

....

....

....

....

....

....

....

....

....

....

....

....

....

CAREER TROLLS

———

As in the story about the ugly troll who prevented passersby from crossing his bridge, we often encounter obstacles on our career journeys as well. These obstacles may not be huge ugly creatures, but they can be just as frightening. These are *emotional trolls*. They are the images and anxieties we sometimes create in our heads when we're faced with change. The more upset we get about the change, the more ominous these emotional trolls become. James Brewer conjured these emotional trolls in his own mind—thus blocking his progress across the bridges of his organization's changes. And as he found himself on the other side of change, looking across at others who were progressing on their career journeys, he wondered why he got left behind.

1. Do you have similar emotional trolls concerning organizational change in your own mind? If so, how would you describe these trolls?

....

....

....

....

....

2. How can you eliminate these emotional trolls—in other words, push them off the career bridges as you pass?

....

....

....

....

....

Chapter 2

Understanding Change

Understanding organizational change is critical. The problem is that the people most affected by change are usually the ones who least understand it. Change may make perfect sense to those who created it, but it may lose most of its meaning as it is implemented throughout the organization. The first thing you must understand is who created the change. Let's call these people the *change initiators*. These are the people responsible for discovering the need to change and then acting upon this need. As their name implies, they must initiate change. They set the ball in motion. But the initiators are usually not the ones who are charged with the responsibility of actually implementing the changes. These people are the *change implementors*. Finally, there are those the changes are intended to affect: the *change targets*. Although everyone's role in the organization will be affected by the new changes, the change targets are the ones who will receive the full impact. But what is intended and what actually occurs, of course, can become two distinctly different things. We'll be exploring this disconnect between desired outcomes and reality throughout the book.

Initiators, Implementors, and Targets

The relationship between change initiators, change implementors, and change targets is illustrated in Figure 1. This book is basically designed to help the change targets. Nevertheless, change initiators and implementors will find valuable lessons about the perspective of those who are most affected by their actions. Not only that, but it's entirely possible that change implementors as well as change initiators may someday find themselves in the role of change targets.

One of the major differences between these three groups is the element of time—that is, when they become aware of the next change (Figure 2). Obviously the initiators are the first to know about changes as they are the ones who create them. Next, the initiators pass the responsibility of the change to the implementors, making them the next to know. Finally, the targets learn what has been planned for them. They are at the bottom of the information chain. The problem with these differences in timing is that by the time the targets hear about the change, the initiators are already thinking about the next change and may not be sensitive to the turbulent emotions the change may be creating. It isn't that the initiators don't experience these feelings. It's just that they already went through these emotions when they were directly involved in initiating the change process and have now moved on to something else. Thus the initiators may be insensitive to the needs of the targets as the changes are announced. They probably don't mean any harm or disrespect. They're just worrying about the next change coming around the corner, not thinking about the last one.

Understanding organizational change requires not just knowing where it comes from but what it's really all about. Let's turn to some of the things you should be asking or doing as the process of organizational change begins.

Figure 1. Relationship Between Change Initiators, Change Implementors, and Change Targets

1. Change Initiators
Those who design and begin the change process

↓

2. Change Implementors
Those responsible for implementing the changes

↓

3. Change Targets
Those most directly affected by the changes

Learn As Much As You Can

Ask questions; read what is sent out about the changes; observe what is happening. Try to identify the initiators and the implementors. The implementors are usually easy to spot—they are probably the ones telling you about the changes. The initiators may not be so obvious. They may be the implementors' bosses, but not necessarily. There could be other *influencers*—yet another category in our cast of characters affecting organizational change. As their name implies, influencers can have a major impact on what ultimately happens throughout the organization. Influencers cause the initiators to act. The most significant thing about influencers is that they may not even be part of the organization. They can be outside influences. They may be not a single individual but a segment of the general population at large—such as customers—or even something as remote as a foreign economy. Once you have a better understanding of what's driving the change, you can begin to appreciate how it will affect you. These are very important things to learn.

Figure 2. Timing of Learning About Change

1. Change Initiators
Because they create the change, they are the first to know about it

2. Change Implementors
Next to learn about change, they are charged with the responsibility to implement it

3. Change Targets
The last to learn about the change

Time

Talk to as many people as possible to gain their views about the change. Find out what or who are the influencers driving the organizational changes. Listen carefully to everything being said about the change. Learn as much as you can. Again, this is particularly important during the earliest stages of organizational change. Sometimes the rationale given for the change loses its meaning as it is presented again and again or filtered for the public. The early stages are the best (and possibly the only) time to really understand who are the influencers and initiators of the changes.

Listen to the Buzz About Reorganization

The best thing to do, particularly in the earliest stages of the change, is to soak it all up. Pay attention not only to what is being said but to *how* it is being said. You can usually tell how people really feel about something by how they say things. Those who are being convinced against their will have not abandoned their original opinion. In other words, their hearts may not be in the implementation of the changes, and it will show. Listen for the buzz throughout the organization about how different people feel about the changes. These can be important signs of how these changes are going to be implemented and by whom. In this buzz, you can gain insights into the real influencers and initiators of the change. All this is important to understanding how you can deal positively with the changes taking place. As we will see in Chapter 7, organizational change is much like a political process. There are factions, for example, struggling for power and position as everything begins to get realigned. And some of these factions may have great influence on the eventual outcome of the changes. Listen carefully to what is being talked about informally to learn what's driving these influencers.

Pay Attention to the Rationale

What does management expect to achieve with these changes? Are there hidden agendas? A hidden agenda is an objective that is not clearly stated up front—sort of a subplot or behind-the-scenes activity that occurs during organizational change. Be aware that what is officially being presented as the rationale for the change may represent only part of what management really hopes to achieve. This is where things get really interesting. Look for inconsistencies among the initiators of the changes. Is what they say the true rationale for the changes? Or are they offering explanations that just don't make sense? You may hear very vague reasons or even counterproductive rationales for the change. When you hear these, you can safely assume there is some other reason that is not being stated publicly.

Take, for example, the official reason for a major change in a sales organization in a large corporation: "In order to better serve our rapidly expanding customer base, we are realigning our sales organization to be able to meet this objective. A new organizational reporting chart is attached." Sounds pretty logical, right? But the attached reporting chart shows a significant reduction in the number of salespeople in the new organization. If you were affected by this change, surely you'd ask yourself: "Is this reorganization really about trying to serve the customer better? Or is it about reducing the number of people in our sales force? Is the real purpose for this change to cut operating costs?" It's entirely possible, of course, that a smaller, more efficient sales force may indeed serve the customer better. But if this is the case, why wasn't this stated as the objective of the changes being made?

This is an important point that everyone, particularly those who sponsor changes, must understand as they are introduced. If you want everyone in the organization to support the changes, they have to understand the true objectives of the changes. Remember the Duck Test? If it looks like a duck, sounds like a duck, and smells like a duck then it's probably a duck. People know a duck when they see one. Similarly, people know the difference between an initiative to get closer to the customer and a cost-cutting effort.

Is the Reorganization About People or Process?

If the change is about people, it was probably designed to give certain people either more or less responsibility. If it's about process, certain functions of the organization will be changed. This is where the subtleties of organizational change come into play. Sometimes the purpose may be clearly stated as an effort to develop certain people for future assignments. Sometimes, however, the purpose is a little harder to decipher. Process changes may involve different personnel assignments, but their main purpose is to make something operate more efficiently. This is one circumstance where the "if it ain't broke" principle may actually be useful. If there's no problem being addressed by the change, then it's likely the change is about people. But if there is a problem that's being addressed, then it's likely the change is about process.

In either case, you'll have an excellent glimpse into the long-term strategy of leadership through their stated objectives. In these messages may be their plans for people and processes in the future. This can tell you a great deal about where the organization is headed. Perhaps there's a new process being implemented that you may want to learn a great deal more about. Or perhaps the initiators in the organization are about to introduce change once again. It only makes sense that you'd want to know the direction the organization is heading and how it may affect you.

Reorganization in Disguise

Sometime reorganizations are camouflaged. This may be done for any number of reasons—not wanting to upset people, for example, or wishing to downplay the change's emotional impact. Whatever it's called, a reorganization is still a reorganization. The difficulty is that this isn't like the Duck Test. Although it doesn't look like a duck, sound like a duck, or smell like a duck, it is still a duck! Calling a downsizing by some other name may make it seem less traumatic in the short term or reduce its impact on the public, but ultimately it weakens the credibility of the initiators. The next time they want to introduce a legitimate management change, people may begin to get anxious about their job security or wonder who's going to get the ax next. Actions do speak louder than words. Watch for what actually occurs after a change is announced. Pay attention to the difference between the stated intention of the change and what's really happening. Was there a hidden agenda behind the change? Was it just a way of accomplishing some other objective that nobody wanted to talk about? The better you observe organizational change, the better you'll be able to survive during these important transitions.

Keep in mind that organizational change is a dynamic process that never really ends. A basic survival skill in organizations today must be to learn to deal positively with these constant changes. It's like swimming in an ocean of change. No sooner has one wave of change hit you than another is on its way. If you let the first wave knock you down, you risk being drowned by the next one. But if you learn to ride the first wave, the second will propel you even farther ahead. Just like the ocean, there's unlimited energy and momentum in these changes. You need to learn to move in the same direction as this energy, rather than crashing against it and being knocked down. This may not always be easy. You may desperately want things to stay the way they are right now. You may have just gotten used to the last wave of change. Maybe you don't feel ready for the next one. But resisting organizational change is like trying to stop the tide. You can expend a tremendous amount of energy trying to accomplish this objective, but ultimately you'll have no impact at all on the outcome.

How Good Is Your Radar Screen?

Radar screens enable us to see objects a great distance away—thus giving us advance warning of their approach. These warnings can begin as just a momentary blip on the screen. What if you had a device that could warn you about the next change about to occur in your organization? This marvelous device might be called an early warning radar screen. All you'd have to do is turn it on and look ahead to what's coming at you next.

Sound too good to be true? Maybe not. Actually, you already have such a device if you choose to use it. You have the innate ability to see into the future by using your intuition and reasoning power. Most change gives us some kind of warning that it is about to occur. It's up to us to see these signs. Just like everything else, some people are better than others in utilizing these abilities. The good news is that this is another skill you can learn to help you survive during times of turbulent change.

How good is your radar screen? The greatest challenge is to recognize what we see. At the beginning of World War II, United States military personnel reportedly dismissed the squadron of Japanese planes en route to bomb Pearl Harbor as nothing more than a flock of birds—a disastrous misinterpretation of an image on a radar screen. How clearly can you see the next change coming? Do you pay attention to even the faintest of blips on your radar screen? Or do you just dismiss them as insignificant?

What do some of these blips on your radar screen look like? There's nearly always an indication or just a hint that something different is about to happen. These can be very faint blips, so you have to really pay attention or they can slip past you. Although the first reports of a break-in at the Watergate apartments appeared on the back pages of newspapers in 1972, this blip eventually caused the president of the United States to leave office in disgrace. Or what about the rumor that President Clinton was having an affair with a young White House intern in early 1998? Here are a few examples of how such a blip on your early warning radar screen might warn you of what's possibly on its way:

Blip	Possible Forewarning
Change in company leadership	New strategic business plan that could change the company's entire direction
Loss of a major customer	Reexamination of a number of systems in the organization that affect customer satisfaction
Political or world events	Change in the economy that could directly affect markets and customers
Computer error message	Programming problem that could affect entire operation
Introduction of new technology	Old methods have become obsolete

In Exercise 3, list some potential blips that might appear on your personal radar screen and explore what they could mean.

A Model of Organizational Change

Once it appears on your radar screen, organizational change occurs in various stages and sequences. Learning about these stages will help you be better prepared to welcome change. In the following paragraphs we'll look at a four-stage model outlining the sequence of organizational change.

Stage 1: Change Event Occurs

In Stage 1, some event occurs that changes the status quo in the organization. It might be new technology, changing markets, new regulations, or people in different positions. At first this event may seem insignificant (a momentary blip on the screen), or it may present itself as a major world event. It might be a slight softening of prices for your product during the last quarter, for example, or a sudden downturn in the stock market sending financial panic throughout the world's economic markets. Often it's not the magnitude of the event so much as people's reaction to it. A company's top management may take no action at all after a 300-point drop in the Dow Jones Industrial Average even though it may have an effect on their markets. But they may have a significant

DETECTING BLIPS

What might be some examples of blips on your early warning radar screen?

Blip on the Radar Screen   **Possible Forewarning**

....

....

....

....

....

....

....

....

....

response to corporate profits dropping even slightly during the last quarter. They might respond with cost-cutting programs, new sales and marketing initiatives, cutbacks, and even reorganizations to try to control this problem.

Stage 2: Change Event Causes Dissatisfaction
A result of this change event is dissatisfaction with the way things stand in the organization. The change event may make the current ways of thinking and doing things in the organization obsolete. What used to be the most modern way of doing things suddenly seems archaic and out of date. The need for a new approach is clear. There begins a search to find new ways of dealing with the change event. Sometimes these efforts are public and well defined. At other times

they may not be publicized but are done in secret to prevent competitors from benefiting. Or entrepreneurs may be working on these discoveries out of the mainstream of organizational change. Many of our most significant discoveries in reaction to change are made in this way.

Stage 3: Organizational Change Takes Place

The organization adjusts to the new order of things with changes designed to help adapt to the change event. After all, isn't it the job of management to deal with the changes that face the organization? In the old western movies, the sheriff comes riding in on his white horse with guns ablazing and saves the town from the gunslinging band of dirty thieving outlaws. But today, despite their brave and noble attempts, this sort of management posse may not always restore peace and order. Today people are more likely to feel they are being victimized by the management posse. The villains may appear to be the changes themselves, not the problems that made them necessary in the first place. This is why management must ensure it does a good job of communicating to everyone why these changes are necessary and how everyone will be affected.

There are four phases of organizational change once it begins. The first phase is *confusion*. No matter how well the changes are communicated, there's still an initial period of disorientation throughout the organization as everyone's bearings have changed. This phase can seem like someone took you blindfolded deep into the woods and left you to find your way home. And in a sense that is exactly what happens. Suddenly you find yourself in unfamiliar territory. You have no idea how you got there (or how to get back). But when dealing with organizational change, there is no going home. Where you are is where you will stay—at least for the duration of the change. Again, this is why effective communication is so essential throughout the organization. Imagine how much less traumatic being taken someplace new would be if you were told exactly where you were going, how you would get there, and the various directions you could travel from that point. Isn't this much more reassuring than suddenly being dumped somewhere without explanation? Some degree of confusion is inevitable. But the better the communication about the changes, the less this confusion will be.

The second phase is *adjustment*. Everyone must begin to adjust to the changes. This too can be a very uncomfortable time. It's like trying to get used to a new home you have just moved into. Nothing is where it used to be. Everything that was second nature to you now seems remote or foreign. Instead of knowing exactly where to position the hot and cold water faucets to get the right temperature in the shower in the morning, you're either scalded or frozen as you scramble to make the adjustments. You seem to be going constantly from one extreme to another, not knowing how to find the proper balance. But then you begin to establish new patterns, maybe even more effective ones. You begin to understand how the new system can work for you. You may even discover new features that make your life a little bit better. It's like finally beginning to enjoy the improvements and extra room that your new house provides. You begin to understand why you subjected yourself to such stress and anxiety when you decided to move. You realize that to grow and progress in your life requires such periods of adjustment and that ultimately you'll be happier as a result. You even figure out how to adjust the water temperature in your new shower (and discover it's actually easier to do than it was in the old house).

Functioning follows adjustment. This is the phase when the intended benefits really come to fruition. The kids get used to their new schools, the draperies and pictures get hung, you get to know your new neighbors, your hard work on the lawn pays off with greener grass and fewer weeds, and you finally get a chance to relax in that hammock in the backyard on Saturday afternoon. There's less and less talk about your old home (except, of course, for missing friends and neighbors you left behind). But other than that, the move has become a successful change in your life—even though it entailed some risks. Organizations face this same risk every time they change. It is their hope and intent that the organization will function better as a result of the new changes. Although things may not work out this way, it is always the ultimate goal.

Peak efficiency is the last phase of organizational change. By its very definition, "peak" means that you have reached the top. Once you have reached this pinnacle of success, there's only one place to go: down. Organizations always look at these performance peaks and begin to compare all subsequent performance against this standard. Anything less will be deemed unacceptable. It's only a matter of time before this dissatisfaction leads to action—and the next change is on its way.

Stage 4: Cycle Begins Again

The cycle repeats itself over and over. "The only constant around here is change." This is the way it seems to most employees as one wave of change is soon followed by another and then yet another. Like it or not, the fact is that change will never stop. Resisting it, therefore, is futile. It will only lead to disappointment and failure. It's like swimming against a current so strong that it will quickly exhaust all your energy and sweep you away in its path. Wouldn't it be much more productive to swim with the current and let it carry you along on your way? This requires far less energy and yields much better results. But these currents of change can shift quickly. Going with the flow yesterday may have been different than it is today. An important part of dealing positively with change is understanding which direction it is going.

This may involve preparing for the next change before the last one has run its course. Although this may sound unusual, even premature, thinking strategically about change can put you in a position that makes the next one much easier to accept. Becoming too specialized in your skills, for example, makes the introduction of something new seem more like a threat than an opportunity. But if you take a strategic look at how you can deal with the next wave of changes, you may think of ways you can develop more versatile skills in the future. With this flexibility, the next round of changes won't seem so threatening.

A Formula for Change

Let's look at this model of organizational change as a formula that can help you predict changes as they approach. This formula summarizes how and why change occurs in organizations:

Change Event (CE) x Dissatisfaction (D) = Organizational Change (OC) ⌐

The change event (CE) multiplied by the dissatisfaction (D) creates the organizational change (OC)—and then the cycle repeats itself (⌐). If you use your radar screen to spot the first blips of a change event and then factor in the dissatisfaction this may create, you can begin to envision what organizational change may be on its way. Let's say a new technology has been developed—one that could change the way your entire industry does business. This change might cause dissatisfaction with the current way of doing business. The old technology may be totally noncompetitive with the new. The result of these events is obvious: There must be some kind of change. Either the new technology needs to be adopted in the organization, or the organization needs to change the direction of its business. The new change continues until the next one comes and the cycle begins anew.

Think about some real-life examples of this formula at work. Perhaps one of the best examples is the introduction of the personal computer. This represented a definite *change event,* which in turn created unhappiness with the old way of doing things. Any operation that depended on manual calculations or organization of databases quickly became obsolete as these amazing new machines took over the business world. This definitely created *dissatisfaction* with the former system. It was either adapt to this *organizational change* or perish.

What about other major change events of the past? What dissatisfaction did inventions such as the telephone, automobile, and television create? What about the introduction of the Internet? Do you believe this is a change event of the same magnitude as the introduction of the telephone, television, or automobile? Think about the impact this powerful communication tool will have on future generations. Imagine the impact this change event might have on your own life. What will it do to your shopping habits, communications, and ability to access databases, research information, and the like? What dissatisfaction will this new technology create with the way we have done things in the past?

Use Exercise 4 to explore how you might use the organizational change formula to prepare for upcoming changes in your organization.

Twelve Early Warning Signals

Being able to read the signs that organizational change may be imminent will help you prepare for the new things to come. The following warning signs that organizational change is stirring should be blips to watch for on your early warning radar screen.

Sign 1: Problems Are Not Addressed at Once

A telltale sign is problems in the organization that are left unaddressed or allowed to go on longer than anyone would have expected. "When are they finally going to do something about that?" This is a common question heard around watercoolers throughout the organization as people try to understand why these problems are not being addressed in the usual way. The reason for this delay may be that the change initiators have not yet decided how to deal with the problem in the new scheme of things. To try to solve the problem under the old system would only perpetuate the old ways of thinking and diminish the effectiveness of the new approach.

APPLYING THE FORMULA TO YOUR ORGANIZATION

How can you use the organizational change formula to prepare for the next possible change in your organization? Think about how these components of the formula might apply in your organization:

Change Event (CE)
What change event might occur in your organization?

....

....

Dissatisfaction (D)
What dissatisfaction might this change create?

....

....

Organizational Change (OC)
What changes might occur in the organization as a result?

....

....

Cycle Repeats Itself (↵)
When might the cycle begin anew?

....

....

The Formula
Now fill in these components of the organizational change formula:

CE_____ x _____ D_____ =

OC_____ ↵_____

Sign 2: Key Decisions Are Postponed

Key decisions may be postponed for the same reason. The initiators may be delaying these decisions until their new organizational plan is in place. To make big decisions before these changes are completed could ultimately cause even more confusion than doing nothing. The thinking may go something like this: "Making no decision is better than making a bad decision that will have to be undone after the changes are made." Whether this rationale proves logical or not, only time will tell. Nevertheless, this is often the most attractive alternative for initiators in the midst of planning for the next change.

Sign 3: Positions Are Left Unfilled

Once again, delay is the name of the game. Organizational change often includes new assignments and reporting relationships. Sometimes it involves a complete restructuring. To fill a single position without announcing the entire new organizational plan may be even more of a problem than leaving it vacant for the time being. The way the position is to be filled (and by whom) may make sense only with an understanding of the entire restructuring plan. Again the initiators may be forced into inaction because they are not yet ready to announce the planned changes.

Sign 4: Decisions Don't Seem to Make Sense

If you were privy to all the information the initiators knew, maybe the decisions would make more sense to you. (And then again, maybe not!) Maybe the rationale for these decisions will become clear once the changes are announced. Before that happens, however, people may be scratching their heads wondering what in the world is going on. This is like seeing only one isolated piece of a puzzle before it is fit into its proper place and completes the picture. Alone it may not look like anything familiar. But as part of the completed puzzle, it is clearly seen as an integral part of the bigger picture.

Sign 5: The Rumor Mill Gets Active

Everyone loves a rumor. No matter how hard the organization tries to prevent them, rumors will always be part of organizational change. Information just seems to have a way of "leaking out." And the more sensitive and confidential the information, the greater the chance that it will be leaked. We see this in the news media every day. "Speaking on the basis on anonymity, sources close to the White House have told us that the president did have . . ." And so it goes. People just can't seem to keep their mouths shut when it comes to knowing something that someone else would love to hear. Here is a general rule: If two people know something, then technically it is no longer confidential.

It's dangerous, though, to rely on the rumor mill as your only source of information during times of change. The rumor mill is not always accurate. In fact, it's sometimes very inaccurate as false reports begin circulating throughout the organization. But typically the rumor mill does provide at least a warning signal that change is in the air. There's a little truth in every rumor. And there may be a lot of truth in rumors about organizational changes that may be about to occur. It's a good idea to be aware of what the rumor mill is saying and watch to see if it's right or not.

It's even more interesting to see what those in a position to know might say when confronted with these reports. This can also put them in a classic Catch 22 situation. If they confirm the rumor, they are in essence making an announcement about changes before they are ready—which might jeopardize other information and plans. But if they deny the rumor, they damage their credibility in the future. Middle-of-the-road responses—such as "I can't comment on that at this time"—are tantamount to an unintended confirmation of the rumor as well. There's really no way out of the dilemma once plans for organizational change get circulated prematurely. The longer information about organizational change is kept under wraps, the more active the rumor mill becomes. The only way to beat the rumor mill is to starve it to death. You do this by sharing as much information as you can, as soon as you can, with as many people as possible concerning the changes that are about to take place.

Sign 6: Outsiders Tell You Something Is Going On
Often people outside the organization are the first to know that something is going to change. This may be information that has been shared with them in confidence. (Remember the definition of confidential?) Maybe those who have access to this information felt these outsiders had a business need to know before those in the organization. Perhaps they were just trying to build a stronger relationship with customers by entrusting them with this information and hoping the favor would someday be reciprocated. Maybe they just wanted to talk to someone who was not directly affected by the changes.

Whatever the reason, these outsiders may know something you don't—and they may be bursting at the seams to share it. This is not to say that you can't trust others to keep information confidential. It just means that it's more difficult to manage information once it's been shared with others.

Outsiders may not fully understand the implications of the information. They may not be aware of the personal stakes involved. The point is that these outside contacts may have very reliable information that change is on its way. They may be more than just a blip on your radar screen. They may have an actual eyewitness report of what is about to happen.

Sign 7: Changes Occur in Key People's Behavior

If you know something, it's hard to act like you don't. Those who are planning the change may not even realize they're acting differently as a result of knowing what's about to unfold in the organization. Although they may valiantly try to maintain an image of business as usual in front of everyone, sooner or later there's bound to be a crack in this veneer. Look for unusual reactions to situations from these key people, and remember that they indeed may be the initiators of the next change. If their actions don't really fit the current situation, maybe they're already factoring in what they know about what's coming.

Sign 8: More Closed-Door Meetings Take Place

There used to be a popular country and western song heard frequently on the radio called "Behind Closed Doors." Although the song was describing a somewhat different situation than organizational change, the principle remains the same. The fact that the door is closed means something must be going on inside that room. As most organizations have adopted an open-door policy concerning accessibility to management, these closed doors seem to contradict this policy. But doors do need to be closed during the planning stages of organizational change. Remember, this is a time when rumors have an even greater tendency to spread. To openly discuss confidential matters in these earliest stages of organizational change would only confuse everyone unnecessarily. Some things do need to remain confidential. Information is not only powerful but sometimes dangerous—particularly information concerning organizational change. The initiators are doing the right thing by keeping these discussions to themselves. But an increase in closed-door meetings should be a tipoff that something is in the wind.

Sign 9: Hints Are Offered by Top Management

At some point during the change process, the initiators may want to begin sharing at least some bits of information about the future. They may want to test the waters—to gauge the organization's reaction to the proposed changes. They may also want to lift the shroud of secrecy they've imposed in the initial planning stages. After a while it's hard to find credible ways to disguise your activities and contain this sort of information. At long last they want to come forward and begin setting the course for the organization's future. Even though they may not yet be ready to announce the changes formally, it may now be time to begin setting the stage.

Sign 10: Unusual Visits and Meetings Are Noted
Organizational change sometimes makes strange bedfellows. Planning change in an organization may bring together people whose normal duties don't even place them in the same room. But here they are working together in earnest on some secret project that no one will give you a straight answer about. Seems sort of odd, doesn't it? It may well be a sign that some big change is about to take place.

Sign 11: People Are Asking Unusual Questions
To plan change requires information. It's unlikely the initiators have all the data they need without involving others in the organization. They may need to see technical information, personnel records, and financial reports in order to complete their planning. They may ask others in the organization questions that seem out of context or unusual. The information they request may seem utterly unrelated to any current project. "I wonder why he wanted to know that?" Such questions may be on many people's minds during this stage of the change process.

Sign 12: Answers Regarding the Future Are Evasive
Again, there's a fine line between sharing information prematurely and maintaining your credibility during times of organizational change. The most effective leaders develop the skills necessary to maintain this delicate balance in their communications with employees during times of change. Trust, of course, is essential. If a manager has developed a high degree of trust with employees in the organization, an answer that does not deal directly with the real issue may be accepted and understood. Leaders must be careful, however, not to erode this trust by continually answering questions in such a manner. The greater the trust, the deeper the well. But every well has a bottom and can eventually run dry.

Whenever you hear vague or evasive responses to legitimate questions, it's fair to assume that something is about to change but it's too soon to discuss it. You may have just asked the question the initiators hoped no one would ask until they were ready to answer. The more evasive the reply, the more certain you can be that change is definitely on its way.

Change Finally Arrives

At long last all the uncertainty concerning the impending change is over (stage 3 of the organizational change model begins) and the actual event finally arrives. Everyone's focus is now on dealing with the new order of things to come in the organization. This requires different skills than during the previous period of anticipation about the change. Now people must learn how to deal with the change that is about to occur. Exercise 5 will help you develop these necessary coping skills.

Exercise 5

COPING WITH ORGANIZATIONAL CHANGE

Once you have seen the signs of organizational change, it's important to know what really matters. This exercise is designed to help you understand what should be a top priority during times of organizational change. Rank the following items in order of their importance by assigning 1 to the most important, 2 to the next most important, and so on. If you don't think an item has any particular value concerning organizational change, mark it with an X.

.... Frequent communications
.... Rumor mill
.... Access to top management
.... Explanation of why change is necessary
.... Emotional support
.... Spelling out everyone's new role
.... Honoring the past
.... Goals of the new organization
.... New reporting chart
.... Resistance to change

Answers

Actually, there are no right or wrong answers to this exercise. What really matters depends on the situation and organization. What you listed as the top priorities are what you should set as goals in order to welcome change in your organization. Here are some insights into why the items might or might not be of value:

Frequent communications: People need to know what's going on during periods of change. Too often organizations provide information early in the change process but don't do an adequate job of following up. People need frequent updates as changes are implemented.

Rumor mill: In the absence of regular communications from the organization, the rumor mill may fill the information void. But it will ultimately be of little value and should be marked with an X. Because the rumor mill is mostly inaccurate, it will only confuse the situation and contribute even more to the stress. The more information the organization provides during change, the less active the rumor mill will be.

Access to top management: There may be many questions that can be answered only by top management. Employees will be anxious to hear management's views of the changes that are occurring and what management plans for the future.

Explanation of why change is necessary: Change brings hardship for everyone. People need to understand why it's necessary for them to make these sacrifices. They need to understand why the change is necessary and why things couldn't simply remain as they were. They need to know that the cost was worth the price of change.

Emotional support: Too often the emotional side of change is slighted or ignored. Emotions are not always logical or even rational. Organizations may quickly dismiss the emotional reactions of people affected by change as being frivolous or trivial. These emotions are very important, however, and must be given attention during organizational change.

Spelling out everyone's new roles: One of the key questions employees ask during organizational change is: "What's my new role in the organization?" Often the new roles are not addressed until the later stages of the process. Consequently, it isn't always possible to answer this critical question during the early stages of organizational change. But the earlier the new roles are clarified and communicated, the more comfortable everyone will be during the change.

Honoring the past: At first the past may appear to have little value to the change process. After all, the past is now history. The subject now is new beginnings. But the past will always be important to people. It represents who they were and who they still are today. Although people must let go of the past in order to move forward, they also need to cherish and honor what has been. Thus it's important to allow people to honor their past in ways that will help them move forward in the future.

Goals of the new organization: People need to know the goals of the new organization. If they don't know where the changes are intended to take the organization, they won't be able to support them. Everyone needs to be striving toward the success of the organization's new objectives. But first they must understand what they are.

New reporting chart: Who's "in" and who's "out" in the new organization? This is one of the first things everyone will want to know. The new structure should be communicated as quickly as possible.

Resistance to change: This is another item that should be marked with an X. Resisting change simply makes everyone more frustrated and unhappy with what is in fact inevitable.

Chapter 3

Approaching Career Crossroads

After months of speculation, rumor, uncertainty, and most of all anxiety, the announcement about the organizational change is finally made. Keep in mind that a great deal of scrutiny and planning has gone into this change. Probably the initiators have consulted the best and brightest thinkers in the organization to develop their plan. As a result of all this wisdom, big decisions will be made—decisions about who will benefit from the change in terms of position and influence and, conversely, who will not fare so well. All the secret plotting and planning by the initiators is done. The job has now been turned over to the implementors to put the plan into action. So what happens next?

At this point it's important to stress that not all of the personnel decisions in the new organizational structure have been based solely on merit and capability. Myriad factors are involved in decisions concerning the fate of an employee's career. Although it's probably impossible to look at this situation truly objectively when you're the one affected, try not to take unfavorable decisions personally. This is easier said than done, of course, but there are sound reasons for trying to view the situation in this way. Your emotions—and ultimately your actions—will determine how well you adjust and function in the new organization.

The implementors' first action is typically some kind of announcement. This can be accomplished in many different ways. It may be a letter posted on bulletin boards or sent to each employee via e-mail or more conventional means. It may involve meetings in which the plan is unveiled to everyone. It may be communicated via a video, Intranet, teleconference, or similar innovative technologies available today. Whatever the method used to communicate the change, certain events will follow. Probably the first step will be to notify the "winners." Although you won't hear the words "and the envelope, please . . ." as everyone waits anxiously in tuxedos and expensive evening gowns for these winners to be announced, it will be clear to everyone in the organization who these people are. It also will be abundantly clear who has been overlooked or even demoted as a result of the changes.

There are any number of ways in which people may be notified about the bad news. If they are lucky, they will be notified in person and allowed to vent their emotions. But this is not the most pleasant of tasks for managers to tackle. They may be tempted to avoid this uncomfortable situation. Instead they may take the easier path: no action at all. They may simply allow the news to be learned by those most adversely affected at the same time as everyone else in the organization. Although this is the worst possible way for someone to hear the bad news, this scenario is repeated time and again by initiators and implementors who justify it by citing overloaded schedules and deadlines imposed upon them by the change process itself.

During times of organizational change, you may find yourself at a career crossroads. It all depends on the type of news you hear and how you personally will be affected by the change. This may be a point in your career when you must choose the direction you'll go in the future.

Fight or Flight

Organizational change can bring with it big changes in people's careers. Although there may be circumstances beyond your control, to a great extent the magnitude and implications of these changes are in your hands. The decision really comes down to a matter of fight or flight. Fight means that you commit yourself to accepting change and finding ways to survive. Flight means that you won't even try to adjust to the changes and choose to leave the organization instead.

Either fight or flight can be a good strategy to employ during organizational changes. It depends on you and your situation. You cannot do both, however. If your decision is to stay and fight, then do it. If you decide to leave, then leave. Don't stay with the organization physically and take flight emotionally at the same time. Don't become a "dead career walking" like a condemned prisoner en route to the execution chamber. Either nurture your career in the organization or put it out of its misery.

But don't jump ship without a lifeboat. And don't make empty threats. The statement "I'll quit if you move me to that position" might result in the organization wishing you the best of luck in your new career and sending you off with a handshake and a pat on the back! In the eyes of the implementors, you might become just one less detail to worry about. A miscalculated bluff can take you out of this poker game permanently.

Under some circumstances, flight may be the best course of action. For example, what if you were close enough to retirement to walk to shore—that is, only a few years from eligibility for your pension? The organizational changes might give someone in this situation a financial incentive to retire a little earlier than originally planned. This can be a good thing for everyone—including younger employees who may now move ahead as a result of the vacancy. If the changes involve a reduction in force, there may even be a severance package to help people make the transition to a new job and career. For certain talented people who could find better opportunities with another organization, the reductions may actually present a chance to do with their careers what they've wanted to do for years.

Maybe the changes will force things to happen that ultimately will better serve both the organization and the people who leave. With all the organizational changes taking place today, this is becoming more common. Becoming unemployed as a result of organizational change or restructuring is more the norm than the exception in our current business world. Even the most paternalistic organizations have found themselves viewing the employment relationship differently in terms of commitment. Where there was once an implied policy of employment for life for loyal workers, business conditions have forced organizations to violate this covenant. No longer is length of service enough to secure your position when the organization changes. And employees, in turn, are no longer blindly loyal to the company. Everyone is looking out for his or her own welfare. In this context, unemployment is no longer a badge of dishonor. Explaining your unemployed status to a prospective employer, therefore, is not as ominous as you might fear.

Fight, on the other hand, means that you've decided to stay. But staying is not enough if you're not going to put up the fight that may be necessary to truly succeed in the new organization. To put up this kind of fight may require you to do a number of different things to ensure not only your career survival but your long-term success in the organization. The first step toward this objective should be to learn as much as you can about the changes that are being implemented. What's really behind the corporate rhetoric that's being bandied about the organization regarding these changes? What's the rationale being presented to explain why the change is necessary? Is this rationale more myth than reality?

What does it really mean, for example, when the vice president of human resources makes the statement, "We are restructuring the organization to ensure our long-term growth and competitive position in the future"? This statement could mean just about anything from "We need to get rid of all the deadbeats in our company who have been dragging us down" to "We are promoting everyone to higher, more responsible positions in order to handle all the new business we've brought in." If either of these scenarios were even close to the truth, why wouldn't this vice president of human resources just come out and say it? Why do we have to sift through so much corporate jargon to understand what is being said? There may be several reasons. Maybe the true objectives of the change are not entirely clear to the initiators, much less the implementors. Maybe they've identified the need but not the process for the change. Maybe they're acting more out of instinct than reason. Under these circumstances they may find that sitting back and doing nothing is infinitely worse than implementing a plan that's admittedly imperfect.

The only thing worse than having to go through change is having to face the challenges that lie ahead without making any adjustments or developing any strategies. At a small automotive supply company in the Midwest, for example, one of their best-selling products was made obsolete by a competitor's new ideas and manufacturing process. As the president of the company was explaining to the workforce the reasons why they were losing this business (as well as many of their jobs), one employee stood up and said: "We trusted that management would make the necessary changes to keep us competitive even if those changes weren't popular or easy to implement. You people really let us down. We put our faith in you. We trusted you to do what was right and necessary to keep us in business and keep the paychecks coming in." How would you like to be the one to reply to this employee? This highlights the importance of change—and the consequences of not taking the actions necessary to operate successfully in the business world today.

So if you find that the logic behind the change is a little fuzzy, have patience. Maybe this was the best plan that could be developed in response to a change event that suddenly presented itself without notice. Sometimes it's best to simply give the plan a chance to succeed by supporting it, warts and all. Sometimes it's less important to be able to rationalize change than to support it unconditionally. This is not to say that you should accept everything on blind faith. It's just that there may be times when your support can make the difference between the plan's success and its failure.

Letting Go

Letting go of the past can be one of the hardest aspects of lending your support for change. Remember when you were a kid and you played on that piece of playground equipment that consisted of a series of hanging rings? The object was to grasp a ring in each hand and then let go of the last one as you reached for the next. The hardest part was letting go of one ring not knowing if you were strong enough to make the transition to the next. Organizational change presents a similar challenge. Letting go of the past can seem just as insecure and worrisome. No matter how well you may understand what's ahead, moving away from the familiar can make you feel pretty uncomfortable. But not knowing what's ahead is even worse. It's like reaching for the next ring with your eyes closed. You wouldn't have any idea where to reach. How do you discover the next "career ring" during times of organizational change? What do you do if the next ring isn't in sight? What if it seems to be out of reach? Do you simply drop to the pavement below? Or do you hold on and try to find that elusive next ring? This can be the toughest challenge you'll ever face in your career . . . and possibly the most important.

There are many things you can do to help you find that next ring and continue moving forward in your career—even during times of change. The first step is to talk to as many people as possible on all levels of the organization about their perceptions of the change that may be occurring. How do they see your new role and future? But if you're going to ask them for their honest and candid feedback, you must be prepared to listen. You may need to evaluate whether you've arrived where you want to be at this point in your life—or, if not, how you can get there. You may need to take an honest look at yourself and make sure you're not contributing to your own dissatisfaction with your career development.

Exercise 6, Organizational Change Self-Assessment, is designed to help you look at change objectively. It can help you understand how you got to where you are today and how you can get to where you want to be in the future—all in the context of changes you may be experiencing in your organization. But you'll find this Organizational Change Self-Assessment an excellent learning tool whether you're in the midst of organizational change or not. If there are no big changes currently occurring in your workplace, think of these questions in terms of past events that created change. It's always useful to pause along your career journey and look at a map to see if you're still headed in the right direction.

Logic vs. Emotion

Having completed Exercise 6, you may find this is an excellent time to reflect on your current role in the organization in relation to your goals. Are your answers consistent with your fight or flight decision? Are you and the organization moving in the same direction concerning your goals? Are your goals and long-term objectives compatible enough to keep your working relationship productive for years to come? Before you answer these career-defining questions, there's another distinction you should make concerning your thinking process. Are you basing your career decisions on logic or on emotion?

Logical decisions are based on facts and actual circumstances that are pertinent to the situation. Although they may be subject to interpretation, these facts are real and accepted by everyone. Emotion, on the other hand, is not necessarily based on the facts. It is how people feel about the situation. At times emotional reactions can be very illogical, counterproductive, even destructive. At other times, it's important to heed your intuition. In any case, it's essential to recognize that people often respond emotionally to situations. Emotions will always be

ORGANIZATIONAL CHANGE SELF-ASSESSMENT

———

1. In general, how do you think the change taking place in your workplace will affect your present job and responsibilities?

....

....

....

2. How do you think the change might alter the direction in which your career is headed?

....

....

....

3. What have you done in the past that's improved your ability to adapt to this change?

....

....

....

4. What can you do to improve your ability to adapt to the next changes?

....

....

....

5. How can this change help you achieve your career goals and destinations?

....

....

....

6. How might the change prevent you from reaching your career goals and destinations?

....

....

....

7. What decisions have you been forced to make about your career as a result of changes in the organization?

....

....

....

8. Are you satisfied with how things have turned out? Explain.

....

....

....

9. What are the most valuable career lessons you've learned as a result of change?

....

....

....

10. Are you satisfied with the direction change has taken your career? If not, what can you do to make this situation more acceptable?

....

....

....

part of every decision—including such important life events as deciding if you're going to stay with your present employer or seek a new opportunity elsewhere. Exercise 7 will help you test how well you understand the distinction between using logic and emotion in decision making.

We can combine the fight or flight and logic versus emotion factors in a single matrix. Figure 3 combines these four factors in one model and shows their interrelationships. This model illustrates how either logic or emotion can be part of a fight or flight reaction to organizational change. In reality, of course, there's always some emotion associated with logic, and conversely, some logic is associated with every emotional decision. Similarly, there still may be some flight tendencies when someone decides to fight (and vice versa). But for the sake of clarity, the examples presented here are focused on either one or the other of these dimensions.

In the upper left-hand corner of the matrix you see a fight response based mostly on logic. In this quadrant is an example of how a person with this mind-set might respond to change. The quadrant on the upper right shows a flight tendency based on logic. You can see that in this circumstance the decision to leave the organization is based on the facts as seen from the person's own perspective. In the lower left-hand corner is an emotional fight response. This person has decided to make

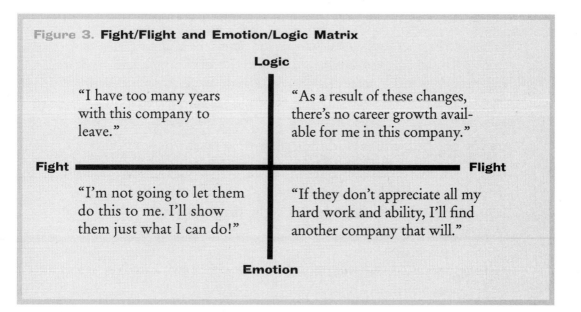

Figure 3. Fight/Flight and Emotion/Logic Matrix

Logic

"I have too many years with this company to leave."

"As a result of these changes, there's no career growth available for me in this company."

Fight — Flight

"I'm not going to let them do this to me. I'll show them just what I can do!"

"If they don't appreciate all my hard work and ability, I'll find another company that will."

Emotion

IS IT LOGIC OR EMOTION?

To help you understand the distinction between logic and emotion in decision making, answer either E (emotion) or L (logic) for each of the following questions to show how the person in the example reacted to changes in the organization.

.... Even though he still has the same job after the reorganization, John is very angry that he was passed over for a newly established position and is threatening to resign.

.... As part of its restructuring, the company has decided to exit a large part of its business in which Alice has spent much of her career. Even though she still has a job despite the downsizing, she decides to seek employment with another organization that can put her experience and expertise to better use.

.... Because her job has been significantly changed as a result of reorganization, Helen has just learned that she'll be required to learn a lot of new skills to continue in her current position. She gets very upset by this and storms into her boss's office to complain about all the time and effort it will take her to learn these new skills.

.... Frank is trying to learn as much as he can about the changes being implemented throughout the organization. He talks to a lot of people on all levels to gain their perspective on the changes taking place. He seeks ways of supporting these changes and understanding his role in the new organizational structure. As a result, he's able to understand the changes as well as his new role.

.... Lou has been hearing rumors lately about some big changes that are going to be implemented in the company. The more he thinks about these changes, the more concerned he gets. He can't sleep at night and becomes more irritable both at work and at home. This begins to affect both the quality of his work and his marriage.

Emotion; Logic; Emotion; Logic; Emotion.

his stand and prove something. In the lower right-hand quadrant, this same emotion can cause someone to feel unappreciated and decide to leave and find a job elsewhere.

The Optimum Balance

Before we leave this subject of logic versus emotion in career crossroads, it's important to emphasize that there are no right or wrong answers. Obviously, you have to balance both logic and emotion in decisions as important as these. Making decisions based solely on logic may seem the right thing to do, but without an emotional appeal there may be no commitment or motivation. If a decision of this magnitude were to be based solely on logic, you'd run the risk of thinking you're doing the "right thing" but still feeling empty and unhappy about it. If decisions are based on emotion alone, however, people may initially have great excitement but quickly lose their enthusiasm if it becomes clear that they're not moving in a logical direction.

Ideally, you should have a balance of emotion and logic in any decision as important as fight or flight. No one else can put himself or herself in your place and tell you how to balance this logic versus emotion dilemma. You must look at these factors and act according to what you think is best for you personally.

Here are a few hints to help you find and maintain this balance of emotion and logic. First of all, put a picture of your family or loved ones on your desk and take a long look at it (emotion). Think about how your decisions might affect them. Then write or update your resume (logic). What kind of career options are available to you? Each of these activities can help put things into perspective and help you make the best decisions at these critical career-defining moments in your life. Use Exercises 8 and 9 on the following pages to explore how well you balance logic and emotion in decision making.

ASSESSING YOUR REACTION TO CHANGE

——

1. How do you think you typically react to change? In what quadrant of the matrix would you place yourself? Why?

....

....

....

....

2. Are you satisfied with the way you'd probably respond to future change? Explain.

....

....

....

....

3. What do you think might be a more productive response given your situation?

....

....

....

....

4. Do you believe you can control how you respond to changes that occur in your personal and professional life? Explain.

....

....

....

....

FINDING YOUR
OPTIMUM BALANCE

———

What's the optimum balance of emotion and logic in career decisions concerning organizational change in your future? Mark an X on the continuum where you think this balance should be:

Emotion ◄————————————————————► **Logic**

1. Is this optimum balance different from your present approach to making career decisions?

....

....

....

2. Think of a time when you relied too heavily on emotion to make a key decision in your life. What was the result? If you had used more logic, how would it have affected the outcome?

....

....

....

3. Now think of a time when you relied too heavily on logic. What was the result? How would using more emotion have affected the outcome?

....

....

....

4. What can you do to achieve optimum balance in making future decisions?

....

....

....

Chapter 4

Exploring the Psychology of Change

Let's turn to an event in history to explore the psychological effects of change. Thanks to the recent blockbuster movie of one of the most famous nights in nautical history, we can experience the virtual reality of what it must have been like aboard the *Titanic* as the impossible began to occur. About midnight on the evening of April 14, 1912, the great ship hit an iceberg in the freezing waters of the North Atlantic and began to sink. How did this change affect those on board that fateful evening?

To help create this analogy, envision the *Titanic* as an organization much the same as the one in which you're employed. There is a definite hierarchy in this organization. The captain is in charge. Under his command are experienced officers reporting directly to him. Moreover, there are employees at many other levels throughout the organization. Those at the highest levels are the most visible, as well as the most vocal, and are provided certain entitlements not afforded those at lower levels. There are others hidden deep in the bowels of the organization who are seldom seen and less often heard. This hierarchy is similar to the stark contrast between the luxurious stateroom accommodations for first-class passengers and those in the steerage compartments. Yet the first-class passengers were just as vulnerable as everyone else when disaster struck. And, as tradition dictates, the captain went down with the ship.

Now think of the waters as time. Usually the organization moves smoothly forward. Everything operates as designed. These waters of time appear calm, even serene. It seems impossible that anything could ever disturb the forward progress of this organization as it steams toward its ultimate destination. But suddenly the serenity is interrupted. Something totally unexpected appears. In keeping with our analogy, let's compare the iceberg to change. Sometimes change creeps up on you. Sometimes it's suddenly in your face. In this case, it was very abrupt.

Just moments before this great ship hit the iceberg, how would you describe the psychological state of the passengers? What were they thinking about? Was it their survival? Probably not. Survival was probably the last thing on their minds, for they had been convinced that the ship was unsinkable. In fact, this mind-set may have responsible for the tragic loss of so many lives that cold April night. If the fact that the ship could indeed sink had been better understood, perhaps more safety precautions would have been taken—including having an adequate number of lifeboats.

Let's say your job is to straighten the chairs on the deck of the *Titanic*. At what point during that evening would these responsibilities have become unnecessary or even illogical? The change event of hitting the iceberg would have caused dissatisfaction—negating the need for this job and just about every other routine of the crew. An organizational change definitely occurred that fateful evening. Nothing was ever the same again. The life of everyone aboard was changed forever. Even shortly after the ship hit the ice, some passengers were still concerned about their comfort and the entitlements they had paid good money to enjoy. They failed to realize there now were more important priorities than having tea served in the comfort of their staterooms.

But as the events of that night began to unfold, it became clear to everyone that the rules of the organization had significantly changed and priorities had shifted. What mattered now was not that coveted first-class ticket and the privileges it afforded but a seat in an open lifeboat in the frigid night air of the North Atlantic—a far cry from the luxuries of just a few short hours before. Wealth and social class no longer had the same meaning. Change can be the great equalizer. People's lives can be so dramatically altered that what they had in the past may be of no use in the future. Several of the richest and most powerful people in the world went down with the *Titanic*. A first-class ticket no more guaranteed someone a seat in a lifeboat than that of a third-class passenger.

The Effects of Change at Work

What have been the psychological effects of change in your workplace, and what influences this collective mind-set? Unlike the passengers on the *Titanic*, people in your organization have more control over their reactions during times of change—or at least they generally have more than two hours to make critical decisions. Who in your organization is most affected by change? Who is least affected? So far, our discussion concerning the change formula (CE × D = OC ↵) has centered on the initiators and implementors of change. But what about the targets? After all, they're the ones the change is being designed to affect most directly. But what is intended and what actually happens are not always the same. The *Titanic,* believed to be the greatest and most unsinkable ship of its time, defied its designers' intentions and did indeed sink—along with more than a thousand people.

How do people react to change? Consider this statement: "I'm all for change so long as it doesn't affect me!" Does it describe how most of the targets feel about change in your organization? What percentage of people are generally in favor of a change and what percentage are against it? What about those who are undecided about how they really feel?

Figure 4 describes how targets generally react to change in their organization. In this model we see that 20 percent of those who are faced with change will resist it. They see themselves as the victims of change. On the opposite end of the spectrum are the 20 percent who will be totally in favor of change and welcome it from the very beginning. They are the most likely to remain successful in the organization as the changes are introduced and implemented. In the middle are those who will accept change but only under certain conditions. About 30 percent of these people will be leaning in favor of change, and another

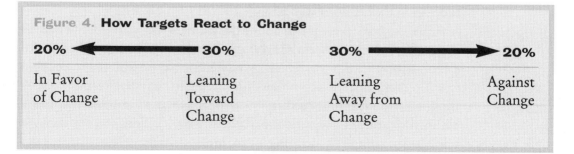

Figure 4. **How Targets React to Change**

20% ⬅ 30%	30% ➡ 20%
In Favor of Change	Leaning Toward Change	Leaning Away from Change	Against Change

30 percent will be leaning against it. Often it's not until the results of the change are known that those in the middle categories commit themselves. Once the results of change are known, you're likely to hear "I knew it wouldn't work" or "I was for it all along."

This is not to say that only 20 percent of the targets in an organization will ever actually welcome change. This is simply how the change targets generally react under most circumstances. The good news is that each of us has the power to choose how we'll react to change. Fortunately, there are no constraints imposed on an organization concerning the percentage of people who feel positive about change and actually welcome its arrival.

Lessons in Change

Let's look at how intentions may turn out to be different from reality as change is introduced in an organization. To give you a better picture of the effects of organizational change, the following examples illustrate how different people might react when actually faced with a change situation.

After what seemed like ages (but in reality was only months), the company finally made the big announcement about the reorganization. It represented the most radical change ever made in the company's seventy-five-year history. Several entirely new functions were created involving new reporting relationships. Although some people thought they were being passed over for certain opportunities, the initial feeling about the reorganization was generally positive. The changes were implemented to create a more streamlined organization—one that could meet the increasing demands of customers and respond more quickly and effectively to their needs. It all sounded great on paper. And if the changes had been implemented more effectively, the results might have been more in line with what was intended.

After the initial optimism about the changes—mostly on the part of the initiators—the process of creating the new organization turned into a bad experience for nearly everyone. Information about the changes was a closely held secret—almost a matter of national security. Only those with an absolute need to know were included in what was being planned (and even they felt mostly in the dark). This secrecy had the unintended effect of creating even more anxiety about the future. Worse yet, those whose responsibilities would be most affected were not informed of their new jobs until just before the reorganization was announced. A few managers first heard about the changes via an e-mail message sent out to everyone on the company's Intranet. Consistent with the company's management philosophy, secrecy was more important than communication—even communicating to people about major changes that were about to occur in their careers.

Once these changes were announced and new positions created, there was still a lot of confusion about everyone's new roles—not to mention resentment over the way these communications had been handled—not a good way to begin a new initiative. Although the initiators had a vision of what kind of organization they wanted to create, they failed to communicate this vision to anyone else. Instead of creating a more efficient organization, the result of the changes was a fragmented and misdirected company that fell far short of its intended goals.

Those in charge of the new functions struggled to understand what they were supposed to do in their redesigned roles. They tried very hard to meet the expectations of the organization in order to make the new system work. But the harder they tried, the worse things seemed to get. They spent most of their time trying to determine what their new roles and interactions were supposed to be. When they asked for guidance, they received only vague generalities from the initiators. Many of them were beginning to shift from the category of leaning toward the change to leaning against it. If this situation continued, they too would begin to feel like victims of change rather than those charged with its successful implementation.

At another company, a new award program was introduced in hopes of improving the organization's lagging performance in the marketplace. The employees of the company were never really told the criteria for this award, however, just that they'd receive one if certain performance targets were met. Instead of working to meet goals for improved performance, they had no choice but to continue doing their jobs as they always had done in the past. It was like shooting at a target blindfolded. Disappointed with their new program's failure to improve the company's performance, the initiators canceled the award program in its first year. As a result, this award initiative caused confusion and mistrust throughout the organization—rather than creating a motivated workforce striving to achieve more challenging team goals in order to remain competitive in the marketplace.

Common Problems

There is a common problem in the inherent design of performance improvement programs. Often they are presented in the form of challenges to the workforce without the support systems necessary to accomplish their goals. What these programs measure is sometimes contrary to the objectives of the initiative. If an organization wishes to improve its safety performance, for example, it might measure the number of injuries reported in a given period of time (monthly, yearly). It might then provide incentives to lower the injury frequency rate—such as shirts, jackets, or caps with safety insignias or even a cash bonus for reaching certain goals. But these incentives might result in an unintended consequence: a reduction in the number of accidents reported rather than everyone working more safely. This can become a vicious cycle. The more the organization rewards its employees for posting better safety records, the more pressure there may be on employees to underreport their injuries.

Another problem is that sometimes we measure statistical variations rather than actual changes in behavior. Safety programs provide another example. Let's say an organization has decided to reduce workplace injuries to a certain level by the end of the quarter in a particular year. Assuming that everything remains basically the same regarding workplace safety and the behavior of the workforce, there really isn't any logical reason for there to be any difference in the results from one quarter to the next. But often there is. There may be many reasons for these differences, but they're probably nothing more than a statistical variation. In other words, there will be quarters when there are more accidents than normally expected and others when there will be fewer. It's the average of the statistical variations that creates the organization's baseline for safety performance. So when the organization celebrates achieving a "safer" performance during a particular calendar quarter, it may be doing nothing more than rewarding everyone for a statistical variation.

What is confusing to the change targets is that they didn't do anything differently this quarter. They just happened to be *luckier* in not getting injured as frequently as last quarter. But the leadership of the organization gets all excited about what they perceive as improved performance and gives everybody a new item of clothing commemorating this significant accomplishment. At one company, as employees were being rewarded with a custom-designed T-shirt to celebrate an excellent quarter of safety performance, one worker was asked if he knew why he was receiving this award. "I don't know," he replied, "but I'm very happy about getting a free T-shirt anyway!" This is a typical response. Everyone gladly accepts a performance award but may not really understand what he or she did to deserve it. Employees may be even more confused about the messages they receive from the change initiators in their organization. One day they may come to work and be rewarded. The next day they may be punished for what they perceive to be exactly the same behavior. Under these circumstances, it's impossible to get the connection between actions and consequences.

Another example is found in the quality process. Virtually every organization has adopted a quality process in one form or another in recent decades in response to our country's eroding reputation for producing high-quality products and services. The basic principle in all these processes is that quality must be considered the paramount goal in all the company's initiatives. These programs often began with much fanfare. Banners and signs began to appear on the walls of organizations bearing slogans such as "Quality Is Number 1." In many operations, particularly in a production environment, it came down to a question of quantity versus quality. In other words, do you ship marginal or even defective products to the customer in order to meet your production quotas? Or do you ensure that everything meets the customer's requirements 100 percent before it leaves your door—even if it costs you the quantity you hoped to reach?

The real test was not in all the hoopla these initiatives created but in the actions of the decision makers in the organization. You can't say one thing is important and then do something completely contrary—not if you expect to have any credibility. If you say that quality needs to be the number one priority, then you have to back it up with your actions—even if it means that instead of reaching a production quota for the month you ensure that customers receive exactly what they expect. What's more, you have to introduce changes that ensure this level of quality is repeated consistently in the future. When everyone in the organization has this basic level of understanding, acceptance of change is at its greatest.

Yet another problem with change initiatives is found when organizations attempt to create internal competition between different departments or segments of their business. The thinking is that this competitive spirit will improve the overall performance of the organization—or "raise the bar," to use a sports metaphor. But unlike a track and field competition, you don't really want there to be winners and losers in your organization. Most of these programs are designed as a win-lose scenario that pits employees against each other. Contests that create such a working environment typically have less cooperation between competing groups— and communication is probably nonexistent. Instead of improving team-work in the organization, these contests may actually extinguish it.

Worse yet, sometimes a group believes that it has no chance of winning and simply gives up. Its members won't help the group ahead of them in the competition, nor will they be motivated to try to catch up. As a result, the contest lowers the performance standard rather than raising it. Wouldn't it make more sense if everyone had the opportunity to win and could reach the desired performance goals? One group's success should not be at the expense of another's. Performance should be measured in a way that rewards team accomplishments, not discourages them. Take, for example, a production environment where you have different crews per-forming essentially the same jobs around the clock. Which would be a better way to measure their performance: on a shift-by-shift basis or in a twenty-four-hour period? If you measure their performance on a shift-by-shift basis, how much teamwork might you expect between produc-tion crews? Probably very little. But if you measure their performance in a twenty-four-hour period, you'll help to create the desired team culture.

Unintended Consequences

Reward systems have another problem experienced by many organi-zations: unintended consequences. Often these programs are introduced with the hope that they'll be the catalyst to create certain changes. But unless they're communicated properly to the targets of change, they'll probably fall woefully short of expectations. Again this underscores the importance of clear communications and clearly defined goals when introducing change. The absence of clarity can create confusion and cause people to lose confidence in the validity and necessity of the change. Everyone needs to understand the intent of the change and what's expected of him or her under the new system.

Stress

Before we conclude this discussion about the psychological effects of change, there's one more important factor to recognize: stress. This factor affects not only the targets of change but also their families and friends. There's no question that change can be extremely stressful. It affects us both physically and emotionally.

Stress can cause people to react in very untypical ways. You might see people displaying behaviors or saying things that are completely out of character. Change can create emotional reactions that would never come to the surface normally—at least not in the workplace where people strive to maintain a professional image. But change can cause people to lose control of their emotions and begin acting on their impulses rather than with logic and reason. These impulses might be called *change bursts*. A change burst is a totally emotional (and often illogical) response to changes at work. As the term implies, these emotions just seem to burst out of someone faced with the stress and pressure that change can create. This is not to say that change bursts are always bad. Sometimes they relieve some of the stress people experience during times of change. But change bursts shouldn't be allowed to become self-destructive. Kicking your wastepaper basket across your office when you're alone may be a good way to relieve the immediate stress related to organizational change. But doing this in front of your entire department is not an appropriate way to vent your emotions. It will only add to your problems rather than help you deal with them more effectively.

Worrying About Change

Most of all, change causes us to worry. We worry about whether we'll still have a job in the future. We worry about having to learn new skills. We worry about moving to another location or another department. Whether the move is to the adjoining desk or across the country, there's bound to be stress and worry.

But how much of what we worry about ever really happens? Most often it's probably less than 20 percent. Often it's the *possibility* of things happening that causes us more stress and worry than the event itself. The worst thing initiators can do to the targets of change is drag out the announcement and implementation of a change that's going to occur. It's the anticipation and fear of the unknown that are usually the worst part of the entire process of change. The longer things go unanswered, the more ominous they begin to seem in people's perceptions. And the rumor mill doesn't help. The more time people have to speculate about what's going to happen, the more creative and even bizarre the rumors become—creating even more anxiety and apprehension for everyone. Exercises 10 and 11 on the following pages will help you take a realistic look at how much you worry and to what effect.

YOUR WORRY INDEX

The Worry Index is designed to help you understand how much time you spend worrying about things related to change in your life—as well as the results of all this worry. For each of the following questions, circle the number that corresponds to your degree of worry.

1. Approximately how much time do you spend each day worrying that things at work might change?

1	2	3	4	5
Less than 1 hour	2–3 hours	4 hours	5–6 hours	8 or more hours

2. To what extent does this worrying affect your job performance?

1	2	3	4	5
Not at all	Slightly	Moderately	Considerably	Very strongly

3. How does your concern about changes at work affect your home life?

1	2	3	4	5
Not at all	Slightly	Moderately	Considerably	Very strongly

4. How does worry about changes at work affect your overall physical health?

1	2	3	4	5
Not at all	Slightly	Moderately	Considerably	Very strongly

5. When you stop and think about it, how much of what you worry about actually happens?

1	2	3	4	5
Nothing	A few things	About half	Most of it	Everything

Interpreting Your Worry Index

Add up the numbers corresponding to your answers. If you scored 15 or less, you worry about an average amount (and your worrying is nothing to worry about). A score of 15 to 24 indicates that you're probably worrying much more than you should. If you scored 25, you need to explore what's causing you so much worry—and what you can do to address these concerns about changes that are occurring in your work life.

1. Do you think you spend too much time worrying about things that never actually happen? Explain.

....

....

....

....

2. How productive is your worrying?

....

....

....

3. How counterproductive is it?

....

....

....

....

YOUR WORRY LOG

—

Try completing this Worry Log during the next week at work. The Worry Log is designed to help you see how much of what you worry about actually comes true. In column 1, simply record something you're currently worried about happening during the next week. In column 2, record the outcome after the week has passed. In column 3, indicate how legitimate your worries were by indicating whether they became a reality or not. In column 4, calculate what percentage of your worries actually came true.

Worry Log

Your main worries at start of the week beginning _____	Actual outcome of these worries	Did these worries become reality? (Yes or No)	Percentage of worries that came true

Where Does Worry Get You?

Worrying about change can affect us physically as well as emotionally. Moreover, it affects people in different ways. Some people don't seem to be fazed by change in any way, at least not judged by outside appearances. But this may not always be the case on the inside. Yet where does the worry get you?

The following chapters will give you more insight into how you can deal with these changes and their effects on you. Reducing the amount of worry and stress you experience as a result of organizational change can be one of the most important things you do to handle change in the future. Who knows, you may even learn to look forward to change.

Chapter 5

Creating Changes in Attitude

Figure 5 on page 64 depicts the hierarchy of change: the five stages of adjustment people experience when introduced to major organizational change. As this hierarchy shows, reaching the highest level involves much more than merely *surviving* change—that is, remaining employed with the organization but staying unchanged yourself. Learning to deal with change involves *adapting* to what has just been introduced. In this learning process you need to develop not only the skills but also the *understanding* of what it takes to remain successful despite all the changes that may be occurring. Dealing with change ultimately means *accepting* new methods, procedures, rules, structures, and people as they are introduced into the organization. The final stage, *welcoming* change, can help you in both your personal and professional life.

Surviving might be compared to someone desperately holding onto a tiny branch to keep from falling down a cliff. Welcomers, by contrast, could be described as pulling themselves back up onto their feet and climbing to the top of the mountain, ready for the next challenge. There is no doubt that experiencing organizational change can seem more like surviving than anything else—particularly during the earliest stages. In a very real sense, organizational change does create survivors. Depending on their circumstances and perspective, there also may be those who are not so fortunate, just as aboard the *Titanic.*

Organizational change can seem like a catastrophic event, especially to those whose lives and careers are hit hard. To understand the stress of change, here's a mental exercise you can do to gain a better sense of what's occurring for everyone in the organization during times of change. Imagine that you're flying over a disaster zone immediately after the event (say a hurricane) has occurred. What are some of the things you might observe? What are some of the short-term needs of the people as they adapt to what's just happened? What are their long-term needs? What communications would be critical to help people understand the situation? What would they need to know to begin to accept the changes? Finally, what could be done to ensure that they welcome the help that will be provided?

To a great extent, those going through organizational change have similar issues. They have both short-term and long-term needs. They desperately need reliable communications in order to adapt to, understand, accept, and ultimately welcome change. They need to know what's going on and what to expect next.

Those who welcome change will ultimately be the fittest survivors. But in this case it's your *emotional fitness* that matters. The best way to prepare yourself emotionally to meet the challenges ahead is to have a positive attitude about change. An attitude of *welcoming* change, not just surviving it, can be the key to your continued success in today's turbulent world.

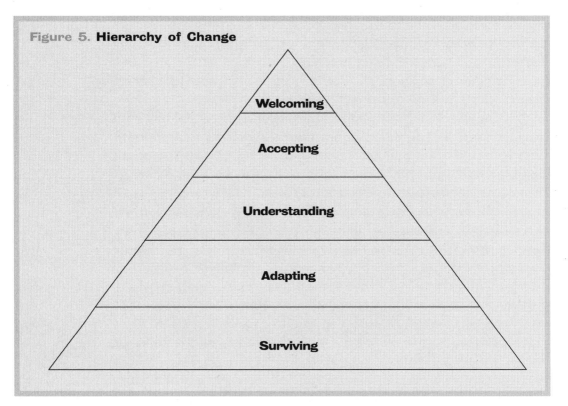

Figure 5. **Hierarchy of Change**

Welcoming

Accepting

Understanding

Adapting

Surviving

What emotions do employees typically experience during times of organizational change? Do they feel like victims of a catastrophe? Are they angry, aggressive, passive, skeptical? Or might they experience all these feelings at the same time? People who are struck by something completely out of their control often feel like victims. But a victim mentality does not usually serve either the employees or the organization very well. Feeling like a victim causes people to give up. The main difference between victims and welcomers of change is their perspective. Victims feel helpless; welcomers feel they need to help themselves. Victims focus on what happened to them; welcomers focus on what they'll do about it. Victims accept whatever happens next; welcomers determine their own future. Which do you want to be: a victim of change or a welcomer? The choice is yours.

Four Stages of Response

How do people respond to change when it's introduced? The four stages of responding to change (Figure 6), unlike those of the hierarchy of change, are not necessarily within our control. They are simply ways in which we typically respond to change.

Reacting

People react to change in different ways. One person's reaction might be very emotional. Depending on how they are affected, people may be elated about the change or devastated. How you react initially may influence your other three responses to the change. An extremely angry response to change, for example, may impede the progress of these other stages.

Refocusing

Change always requires a refocusing of attention and even perceptions. It means that you need to see things differently, operate in your work environment differently, even think differently. This can be an energy-draining experience. Note the shading in Figure 6 in the arrow representing this refocusing. It is less intense than in the other three arrows.

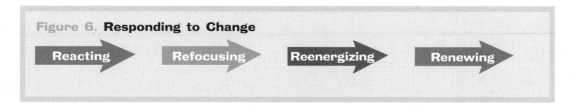

Figure 6. **Responding to Change**

Reacting   Refocusing   Reenergizing   Renewing

This represents the way a person's energy level decreases during this stage. It is during this stage that people need the most support and guidance to focus in the right direction.

Reenergizing

As people begin to understand the changes and their new roles, they find new energy—as shown by the increased shading in this arrow. They begin working to find ways to make the change succeed. There's less focus on the old and a newfound concentration on where things are headed. Instead of investing their energy in clinging to the past, they begin to look forward. They begin to see the possibilities the changes can introduce. They may even try the change on for size to see if it fits. They've begun to cross the threshold between what was and the way things will be in the future. Much of the energy they lost in the refocusing stage begins to return as they stop resisting the change and begin looking forward to what it might bring.

Renewing

In the renewing stage, the organization's energy is at the same level it was at the beginning. The changes have become the accepted way of doing things. This sets the stage for the cycle to begin again. When the next change comes, there may be the same cycle of reacting, refocusing, reenergizing, and renewing as the process repeats itself. And because there is now so much energy moving in the direction of the last change, the next change often meets the same resistance encountered earlier. Redirecting this momentum can be like trying to stop a locomotive. It doesn't take a superhero to introduce the next change. But it may take a great deal of courage and strength to make it work and help everyone learn to accept its arrival.

Although we can't always choose how we respond to change, understanding this process can ultimately help us decide what our attitude will be. In other words, you may not be able to control your response to change, but you can control your attitude about it.

What's Your Change Attitude?

When it comes to dealing with change, attitude is everything. Having a positive attitude about the changes that are occurring can make a tremendous difference. Changing your attitude can be like switching channels on your television set. If you don't like what you see, just switch to a channel that you enjoy. Why would you want to continue watching something that makes you feel bad? Having a negative attitude can be much the same—not only for yourself but for the others working around you. Having to work with someone with a bad attitude is like being forced to watch a program you don't enjoy, day after day, week after week. Unfortunately, others don't have a remote control to switch the channel to something more positive when they have to deal with you and your negative attitude. Only you have control over your attitude. When you think about it, it takes no more effort to have a positive attitude than a negative one—maybe even less.

Your attitude can be your best defense against fear. Ask yourself this question: "Would I rather be on a team with a winning attitude but less talent or a team with more ability but a poor attitude?" Which team do you think has the greater chance of success?

What kind of attitude would you want your coworkers to have? It's really no different than on a sports team. Would you want to work with someone who has nothing more than a survival attitude and is just doing what's absolutely necessary to get by? Probably not—and neither do the people who work with *you*.

The funny thing about attitudes is that we can see other people's attitudes much more clearly than our own. This is particularly true when it comes to bad attitudes. Everyone else might be commenting about Frank's poor attitude, but Frank himself may be oblivious to the problem. Sometimes we need to take a look at ourselves to understand how others perceive us. This introspective look should begin with a personal assessment. Exercise 12, Your Change Attitude, can help you gain this understanding and see yourself as others do.

Changing Your Attitude

Are you satisfied with the way you scored on your self-assessment? If you don't like your score, you probably have lots of company. Now let's look at some ways to help you change your attitude.

Admit You Have a Problem

Admitting that you have a problem, of course, is always the first step in solving it. And when it comes to admitting that we really don't like change, we tend to deny it. People often view change as fine so long as it's happening to someone else. Go ahead and admit it: you really don't

YOUR CHANGE ATTITUDE

Sometimes it's hard to see our own attitude clearly. The following self-assessment is designed to help you understand your attitude as seen by others in the organization. For each question, circle the number that best reflects your attitude.

How often do you find yourself engaged in conversation with others in the organization complaining about recent changes?
1. Daily
2. Weekly
3. Occasionally
4. Seldom
5. Never

How often do you complain to your boss about changes being implemented?
1. Daily
2. Weekly
3. Occasionally
4. Seldom
5. Never

How often do you make suggestions to help implement changes at work?
1. Never
2. Seldom
3. Occasionally
4. Frequently
5. Regularly

How often do you speak positively about the changes being made?

1. Never
2. Seldom
3. Occasionally
4. Frequently
5. Regularly

How often do you try to make changes work better even when you're more comfortable doing things the old way?

1. Never
2. Seldom
3. Occasionally
4. Frequently
5. Regularly

How often are you seen by others as an innovator and one of the first to try something new?

1. Never
2. Seldom
3. Occasionally
4. Frequently
5. Regularly

At what point during the implementation of change in your organization do you find yourself really accepting it and helping to make it work?

1. Only when I have no other choice
2. When I see everyone else adapting
3. After I've seen if the change will work
4. Shortly after it's introduced
5. As soon as it's introduced

Given the choice between changing or keeping things the same, what would you do?

    1. Keep things exactly as they are.

    2. Change only after I'm convinced that the new way will be better.

    3. Wait and see what the new changes involve before making a commitment.

    4. Consider making the change after thinking about it for a day or two.

    5. Try the new way right away.

Which do you value more: tradition or innovation?

    1. If given the choice, I'd choose the traditional way every time.

    2. I tend to stay with what's proved successful over time.

    3. It depends on the situation.

    4. I think innovation leads to growth and development.

    5. If given the choice, I'd look for the most innovative way of doing things.

How would you describe your attitude toward change?

    1. I hate it.

    2. I'm skeptical and usually resistant.

    3. I'm neutral. I go with the flow.

    4. I know that change is inevitable.

    5. I think change is synonymous with progress.

Scoring

Add up the numbers you've circled. Here's what your total score signifies:

41–50   You are truly a champion of change.

31–40   You are moving toward accepting change.

21–30   You could be persuaded to change.

11–20   You are very skeptical when it comes to change.

 1–10   You definitely hate change.

like change. Now doesn't it feel better to finally get that off your chest? You might even share this fact with your friends, coworkers, and family. But be prepared to hear them say that although this may be a revelation to you, it comes as absolutely no surprise to them. We're often the last to realize things about ourselves that have been blatantly obvious to everyone else for a long time.

Seek Help

After admitting that you have a problem with your attitude about change, the next step might be to seek help. You might even go to a "change shrink." A change shrink doesn't necessarily have a degree in psychology or any professional credentials. A change shrink can be anyone whose opinion you trust who can give you advice about learning to change your attitude toward change. Again, you may need to prepare yourself to hear some fairly candid feedback about how you've dealt with change in the past. Simply accept this feedback as the truth and begin to work on your attitude from this point. You may find it helpful to set goals for yourself. What would you like your change attitude to be in the future? You might set short-term goals to reflect your progress in changing your attitude as you move toward your long-range goals for dealing with change in the future.

Quit Complaining

With so many people going around saying negative things about change all the time, no wonder it gets such a bad name. Maybe this is why it's often so hard to understand. Many people derive great satisfaction from complaining about change. They whisper about it during breaks and around the water cooler at work. They show it no respect in their snide and cutting remarks. But what effect does all of this negative talk have on people's attitudes about change? On *your* attitude? Obviously it spreads this negative attitude about change throughout the organization like an epidemic—for negativism can be extremely contagious. The only cure for this negative ailment is to stop complaining about change. Changing your attitude often begins with how you talk about something. Saying positive things leads to positive thoughts and then to positive attitudes. In this way you can change not only your own attitude about change but the attitudes of others as well.

Give Change a Chance

There's another old saying that's still good advice about your attitude: "Don't put something down until you have first picked it up." In other words, you shouldn't judge something you don't really understand. Just because something is new or different doesn't necessarily mean you should oppose it. Some people resist change for no apparent reason. They're against change just because it's different from what they've grown accustomed to. But how do they know whether the change is good for them or not if they never give it a fair chance? Give yourself the opportunity to actually like the change that's being introduced in your workplace. It just might turn out to be one of the best things that's happened to you.

Initiate Change Yourself

What people seem to dislike most about change is the feeling of helplessness it often brings. They may feel that the change is being imposed upon them. They may feel they are being given no say about whether they want it or not. But change is inevitable. No power on earth can prevent it from happening. Even if you sit back and do nothing, change will eventually become a certainty. But rather than just sitting back and waiting for it to happen, you can choose to initiate change yourself. The major advantage of this proactive approach is that it can put you in control of certain aspects of change. For one thing, you may have more say in when and how the change is to be implemented. This is important. It's always better to set your agenda and timetable yourself than to have them imposed on you. This sense of control can become an important factor in your feelings about change.

Discovering the Organization's Impression of You

Your attitude will determine not only how you view the changes but how the new organization views you. Your future may depend on how others in key roles perceive you. Fair or not, often your career may be determined by bits and pieces of information about you. Your entire past career as well as your future with the organization may be reduced to a single comment made by someone who has limited knowledge of your ability and potential. All he or she may see is your attitude toward change and the behavior it creates. Thus how others perceive you and your attitude is very important. Once it becomes part of the organization's collective impression of you, this image can be very difficult to change. It's almost as if it becomes inscribed on stone tablets that the organization keeps on each of its employees.

Your only remedy is to learn how to alter any unfavorable impression the organization may have of you. Almost nothing you can do will have a greater effect on the organization's collective impression of you than changing your attitude. Listen carefully to the advice of others. They may be telling you how others perceive you and how you can improve your image. You may need to take an introspective look at yourself and your attitude. But at the same time you shouldn't automatically accept everything people say about you. Don't make them right about you. In other words, don't make it a self-fulfilling prophecy where you inadvertently make undesirable consequences come true. It's like saying, "If that's how you feel about me after all these years, I'm not going to bother to change it. I'll just do whatever I have to from now on and nothing more!" What kind of attitude do you think this viewpoint projects to others?

Let's say you find yourself in the midst of organizational change. As a result, you realize that your career is no longer headed in the direction you want it to go. You also realize that the organization's collective impression of you is not what you want it to be. What should you do? The following story concerns a young manager who found herself in this very predicament. As you read about what happened to her, think about the accuracy of your own self-perceptions and your organization's collective impression of you—and how it might be influenced.

Mary Cramer had worked for ZenTec Corporation for nearly ten years when the company went through its first major reorganization. Mary felt she had done well in her career at ZenTec. She had progressed rapidly through a number of lower-level management positions as the company gained a better understanding of her abilities and potential. Mary had recently been given primary responsibility for managing a small but growing part of ZenTec's business. Under her leadership the business was at last beginning to break even. Everyone seemed confident that in time Mary would turn it into a profitable business. Most believed that Mary had great management potential and would progress in her career through the ranks to more senior positions in the future. She seemed to have it all: experience, education, motivation, and, most important, attitude.

But change can cause unexpected things to happen. ZenTec's executive committee decided to sell this part of their business that Mary was managing rather than invest the capital necessary to make it profitable in the future. Although the buyers wanted the key managers of this business to work for them as part of the deal, ZenTec insisted on the right to retain any of its employees. Thus important decisions about people had to be made quickly—including what to do about Mary.

ZenTec's executive board, which also served as its management development committee, hastily arranged a meeting to discuss the divestiture of this part of their business. After reviewing all the financial matters pertaining to this sale, their attention turned to the personnel. Who did they want to keep and who would they allow to sign on with the buyers? The buyers wanted to hire the key managers who were most familiar with the operation of this business. They were particularly interested in offering Mary a job like the one she presently held with ZenTec. This issue was now before the committee. What would happen to Mary?

Those who knew Mary and had worked closest with her over the years were the first to speak. What this committee needed to do, they said, was inform the buyers that Mary was not available. The overall consensus seemed to be that she was an extremely talented young manager with an excellent future. But there was one dissenting voice in the group. Frank Hawkins was vice president of finance for ZenTec and had been with the company since its inception nearly three decades earlier. Over the top of his reading glasses he had listened patiently to all the glowing testimonials being made about Mary. Early in her career Mary had reported to Hawkins. This in itself was not unusual. Over the years, many of ZenTec's executives had at one time or another worked for him as part of their development. Regardless of their position, ZenTec believed that its managers should have at least some experience in the financial side of the business. Even the current CEO of ZenTec had started his career many years before in an entry-level position reporting to Hawkins.

As the most senior member of this committee, Frank Hawkins' opinion carried a great deal of weight. It wasn't that Hawkins didn't respect Mary's work and accomplishments. Nor could he cite any specific instances when Mary had done less than acceptable work—even in her first position as a trainee in his part of the organization. His reservations about Mary, rather, were based on an overall impression. Strangely, he wasn't able to articulate these objections very clearly. Ordinarily he was very clear about why he believed a certain decision should be made, so his ambiguity about Mary confused the rest of the committee. When they asked him to be more specific, he simply said, "I can't think of any actual examples or specific situations. I guess it's more of an overall impression that I have about her." This was a very strange answer coming from someone who was such a stickler for detail and accuracy in financial matters.

Hawkins continued: "I remember when Mary worked for me when she first started with the company. She was hardworking and intelligent and showed good initiative, as I recall. But I just don't see her as having the kind of potential everyone else around this table is saying she has. And you all know that over the years my intuition about these things has been pretty good. As I remember, I had a feeling that Jim Clevens had management potential a number of years ago and just look where he is today!" He then looked directly at Jim, who was now the CEO of Zen-Tec, and everyone laughed in agreement. "As I said, I hate to be the odd man out on most matters we discuss, but I guess that's a role I was born to play. I know I may sound insensitive at times, but I've learned to look at the bottom line on decisions like this. Let me ask you this: Why did we make the decision to sell this part of our business?"

After a few moments of uncomfortable silence, Jim Clevens answered: "Because it wasn't meeting our company's financial goals."

"Exactly," replied Hawkins. "And who is currently responsible for this business?" He was asking what he thought would be a rhetorical question.

"But is that really fair to Mary?" a member asked. "We all knew that if we didn't invest more capital in the business it would never be profitable, and we just decided not to do that. This sounds more like a classic Catch-22 situation than an indictment of Mary's managerial abilities," another committee member replied in rebuttal to Hawkins' logic.

Hawkins replied: "I've learned to look at results rather than all the excuses for not meeting objectives. This is why I feel we might be better off letting Mary go to work for the buyers rather than trying to find her another slot in our organization. We have a number of other people we need to decide on and find new positions for, and this might be a chance to relieve some of the pressure. Besides, the buyers are pushing us to let them keep more of our people as part of the deal. They're already upset about several other people they wanted who are going to stay with ZenTec. I don't want to see any more problems with this deal. We need this sale to be able to finance several other important projects we have planned for next year."

This short story about Mary and the organization's collective impression of her illustrates just how quickly your entire future can change. As seen in this story, an organization's collective impression can be greatly influenced by just one person's comment or opinion. Change sometimes moves people toward their desired destination and sometimes in the opposite direction.

What do you think happened to Mary? Answer the questions in Exercise 13 to decide Mary's future.

Changing the Organization's Impression of You

Exercise 14 is designed to help you explore what you know about your organization's collective impression of you. What can you do to change that impression if you're not satisfied that it accurately represents you? The following suggestions can help. But you need to recognize that the organization's collective impression, once formulated, may be extremely tough to change. It may have taken decades to develop, and it won't change overnight. It's like the old saying: "You never get a second chance to make a good first impression." Trying to change a negative impression might seem like you're trying to turn back the hands of time!

Nevertheless, it is done all the time. It may take a significant change event to make it happen. Again, this is one of the benefits of change and shows how it can work for you. Change can be the great equalizer. It can cause organizations to look at everyone in a different way. Sometimes change is the catalyst that allows people to free themselves of the bias and limitations that collective impressions impose on their careers.

Guilt by Association

Are you being lumped together with others in a joint collective impression? This form of stereotyping is common in organizations just as it is in most societies. In these circumstances, the prejudices may be based on a certain part of the organization or even on a single person with whom

DECIDING MARY'S FUTURE

1. What do you think this committee will decide about Mary's future?

_____

_____

_____

_____

2. Do you think the committee should trust Hawkins' "intuition" about Mary?

_____

_____

_____

_____

3. Do you feel that Hawkins' recommendation is fair to Mary? Explain.

_____

_____

_____

_____

4. Do you think Hawkins' recommendation is in the best interest of Zen-Tec? Explain.

_____

_____

_____

_____

ASSESSING YOUR ORGANIZATION'S COLLECTIVE IMPRESSION

———

1. What do you think is your organization's collective impression of you?

....

....

....

....

....

2. How do you think this impression was formed?

....

....

....

....

....

3. Which person was most influential in forming this collective impression?

....

....

....

....

....

4. Was there a particular incident that helped form this collective impression about you? What would this have been?

....

....

....

....

....

5. Do you think this collective impression is accurate? Is it fair? Explain.

....

....

....

....

....

6. How could you determine the accuracy of this impression? Who could you ask for advice?

....

....

....

....

....

A word of caution: If you're going to seek information from various people in your organization, you must be prepared to hear it! You may be getting some very candid feedback about yourself and your career—information that may be upsetting. Remember, you asked for it. Just make sure you use this feedback to help you grow and develop, not to get even or retaliate.

you've been associated. It's a classic case of prejudice: The negative feelings connected to someone or something else are transferred to you. "I don't want anyone in my department who used to work for Johnson. They always seem to learn his bad habits!" This is the way the discussion may go in one of these career-defining moments. Once again, an entire career can be changed by a single thoughtless comment. Being proactive is your best defense against this type of stereotyping. You need to think about ways in which you might be judged "guilty by association."

These associations may not be within your control. You might have no say about what products, processes, and clients you are assigned, much less who you work for in the organization. But you should be aware how these associations may be judged by others. If you come to realize that your present associations will not move you in the direction you want, try to do something about it. If possible, transfer to another job or area that's more conducive to your goals. To the extent that it's possible, distance yourself from these associations. Move on to new opportunities that will allow you to utilize the experience you have gained but at the same time provide you with a new beginning.

Conduct Your Own Opinion Poll

Public opinion polls represent an important barometer of how the general public may be thinking and feeling on key issues. The results of these polls are used to make decisions in both the public and private sectors. Conducting your own public opinion poll of your career and your future might provide you with valuable information and help you make major decisions. Of course, your methods will need to be slightly different from those used by Gallup. People in your organization might not appreciate your calling them at home to ask them a series of questions about your career. If you try this technique during dinnertime, as these pollsters have a bad habit of doing, you may not like what you hear.

Your opinion poll should be much more informal. In fact, it doesn't even have to be obvious that you're conducting a poll. This is information you can collect casually as part of your normal contacts and conversations with others. Ask people in the organization whose opinions you respect to give you feedback concerning your future. Listen carefully to what they say, as their messages may be subtle. Again, you must be prepared to hear what they have to say. If you get defensive and offer a rebuttal, you can be sure you won't be receiving any future feedback from these people. Don't forget to thank them for their input. Don't allow any negative messages they may have given you to affect your relationships with them. And above all, don't become self-destructive. Use this information to help you make change work for you. Learn as much as you can about how others feel about you. Find out the best way to position yourself for the future.

Find Out Who's on Your Side

There's a wise old saying: "Know your enemies." This is especially good advice during times of organizational change. Often the biggest problem in organizations is knowing who's "bad side" you may be on. Your adversaries may be nice to you in person but say less than favorable things about you to others in influential positions—all in the name of management development. Your public opinion poll may tell you who your supporters are as well as your adversaries and why. Understanding the organization's collective impression of you can at least give you a chance to address these issues.

Often the best way to get off other people's hit lists is to avoid having one of your own. There could be a correlation between the two. Take people off your list and you may find that you're removed from theirs as well!

Chapter 6

Getting with the Program

Don't you just hate it when people say "Get with the program!"? What they really mean is that you need to change your attitude toward change. It may appear to them that you're resisting the latest change and becoming an "anchor" opposing its implementation. But it may not be the actual change that you're resisting. Maybe it just hasn't registered yet that a new program has been introduced. It's like dancing to the wrong music at a party. Everyone else may be dancing fast to the latest tunes while you're still slow dancing to a romantic ballad played hours ago. At work you can find yourself so dedicated to working within the old program that you fail to comprehend that it has changed and a new one has taken its place!

A great deal of attention is being paid to the need for organizational alignment—and for good reason. Organizations must ensure that all of their systems support the same overall objective. If not, one part of their efforts may nullify the others. Enormous effort is wasted when such misalignment takes place. When change is introduced, it's essential that it be aligned with the overall direction of the organization. This is the primary objective of most organizational change: to realign everyone's goals in the new direction.

Personal Alignment

Personal alignment means that you as an individual must be aligned with the organization's new direction. Again, this may not always be easy. How do you get with the new program that's being introduced in your organization? The first step is to set a new *personal agenda* for yourself. You need to decide what's of value to the organization now and what has changed. Avoid committing yourself to the wrong things. Don't take a polarized position before you fully understand the issue. Statements like "That idea will never work!" only put you in a lose-lose position that's completely out of alignment with the rest of the organization. If it turns out you were right, you may lose anyway because you could be associated with the failure. If you were wrong and the change is successful, you may be viewed as unable to accept change. Neither of these positions is where you really want to be. Be careful what you wish for. It just might come true.

Figure 7 shows what happens if your personal goals are out of synch with everyone else's. As you can see, these personal goals are way out of alignment. Just think how ineffective this situation is. If your personal objectives are not aligned with those of your organization, your department, or even your job, how can *anyone's* goals be met? Without this

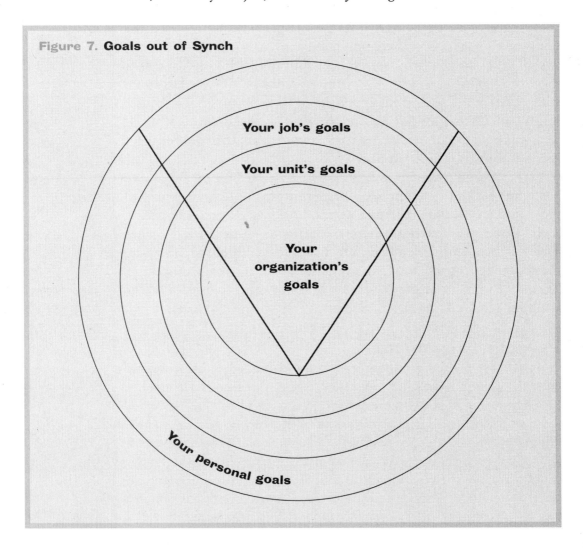

Figure 7. Goals out of Synch

Your job's goals

Your unit's goals

Your organization's goals

Your personal goals

alignment, efforts to reach all these goals are bound to be counterproductive. One effort will negate the other. Goals become mutually exclusive—that is, reaching one goal precludes attaining another. In fact, these goals may actually compete against one another as depicted in Figure 8.

How could such a misalignment occur? Wouldn't you think these opposing goals would have been discovered before and some action taken to correct the situation? Often these cataclysmic differences are a result of change that was introduced without focusing on the goals of everyone in the organization. This is a common problem and a very serious one. Without refocusing everyone's goals with the new overall direction of the organization, you run the risk of having goals that may indeed be canceling each other out.

Say, for example, the organization has decided it wants to change its overall management philosophy. Its former management style was very directive and command-and-control oriented. The new culture will be a more participative style of management allowing greater involvement on all levels in the organization in decision making and problem solving. But suppose management fails to focus on the goals of the individual contributors in this process. What will happen?

The very nature of the company's past management style will make this transition difficult. But if the change effort doesn't focus on the goals of individual contributors, it will be nearly impossible. Employees will try to fulfill what they perceive to be their responsibilities as assigned to them in the past. The mixed messages they receive from the organization concerning this change in overall operating philosophy will only confuse them. For years they were told what to do. Without updated goals in alignment with the organization's new objectives, they'll continue to do their jobs the same way they always have. Even more confusing, the organization may be saying that it wants one thing—in this case, a more participative culture—but it will still be rewarding behavior supporting the old management style. These managers will continue to obey the orders they received when first assigned to their posts. They're like

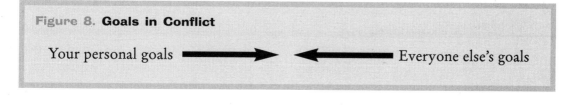

Figure 8. **Goals in Conflict**

Your personal goals ➡️ ⬅️ Everyone else's goals

the Japanese soldiers who were discovered decades after World War II was over still carrying out their mission to hold their position on an isolated South Pacific island until further notice—which, unfortunately, came about twenty years after the war had ended.

The problem is that this old behavior is not what the organization needs. Its employees may indeed understand the new objectives and new direction but have not translated this change into the need for different goals and behaviors. Without this clarity of direction, they will desperately seek reinforcement for the old outdated behavior. When this reinforcement doesn't come, they may conclude they just need to do it "bigger." But increasing the old behavior only makes matters worse. At one company, this caused a manager with many years of experience to find himself on the verge of termination. "I don't understand," he told his boss when confronted about his lagging job performance. "Just a few years ago you told me I was one of the best managers in our division. I performed my job then the same way I do today. Now you're telling me that I'm close to being fired for the same behavior. Why were you so pleased with me then and so unhappy with me now? I haven't changed." The answer was obvious. He hadn't changed. It was his inability to change along with the objectives of the organization that caused him to become ineffective.

Now let's say the organization did a good job of communicating these new objectives and ensured that all the employees understood what was required of them for their goals to be in alignment. What would this look like compared to the alignment models shown earlier? Figure 9 shows everyone's goals in alignment with the direction and current objectives of the organization. There are no mixed messages concerning the individual's goals compared to those of the rest of the organization. The entire system has been designed to achieve the organization's overall goals. The system reinforces behavior that fulfills its employees' personal agendas while moving the organization toward its goals. And no one is expected to be blindly obedient—to carry out orders without understanding what they mean or where they came from.

Expectations

Organizations may have a number of different expectations for their employees. Understanding what someone expects of you can be critical to meeting these goals. Figure 10 shows four of these expectations.

Unspoken Expectations

You can't meet the expectations of the organization if you don't know what they are. Sometimes there are *unspoken expectations* that employees are expected to know but are never told. Although it's not really fair to hold someone to standards you haven't explained to them, this practice is more common than most people realize. Negative evaluations of employees discussed during management development meetings—such as the one in the story about ZenTec concerning Mary—are often the result of that person's failure to meet someone's unspoken expectations.

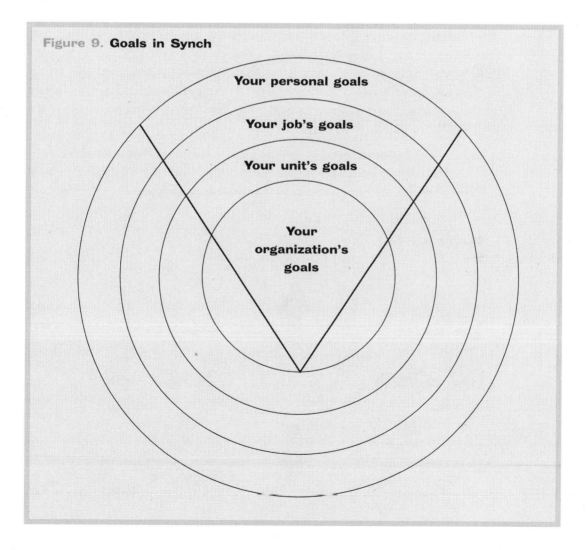

Figure 9. **Goals in Synch**

Your personal goals

Your job's goals

Your unit's goals

Your organization's goals

False Expectations

False expectations are those that people say they want but they don't really mean it. Although they may believe they're supposed to want these things, they're not really committed to achieving them. False expectations result in nothing more than empty compliance—just going through the motions. People may behave in ways they think are expected. For example, employees might wear a quality pin on their lapel but have no dedication to what it symbolizes.

Denied Expectations

Denied expectations are the ones that nobody likes to talk about. These are the hidden agendas. Take, for example, the elimination of a certain part of the organization made obsolete by the new changes. Everyone knows this is expected to happen, but nobody says it. There may even be carefully worded denials by the organization up until the actual event takes palce. Everyone sees through these denials, of course. Despite all the disclaimers and denials, they know what the changes are really intended to accomplish.

Implied Expectations

Implied Expectations are similar to unspoken ones but a little more easily understood. Although still very subtle, at least they are shared with you.

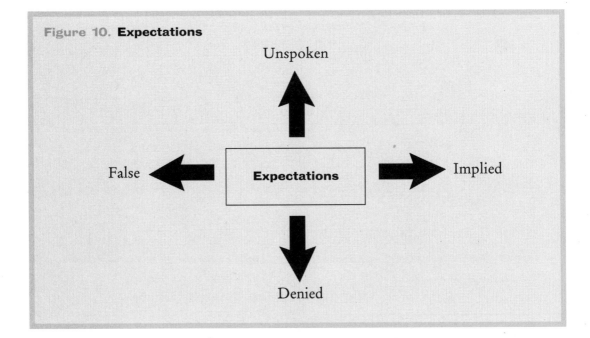

Figure 10. Expectations

But you may have to piece together shreds of evidence that lead you to understand what it is you're expected to accomplish. Obviously you need to listen very carefully to hear these implied expectations—or even realize they're being communicated to you. Moreover, these messages may be transmitted by means other than words. An expectation might be sent to you via a certain decision, for example, or some other change in the organization. Sometimes these implied expectations come as a result of what you *don't* hear, rather than what you hear. Sometimes doing nothing is doing a lot. Sometimes inaction speaks louder than words.

Generally we determine the importance of an initiative by the way it's presented. If the initiative comes with a great deal of corporate hoopla, we tend to pay more attention to it. But if you find that responsibility for introducing a change is being passed down the line in the organization like a bad penny, then its real value is pretty obvious despite all hoopla.

Redefining Competencies

One way of dealing with change in an organization is to find out what is now considered to be of value. Change redefines value. As we saw with the manager who couldn't understand why his company no longer valued his directive management style, this can be very confusing. Even more confusing is the fact that nobody will come running up to explain that the organization's values have just changed. Values in an organization do not change overnight. It is a slow, evolutionary process. Stay alert as this process develops. And stay tuned in to the subtleties of these constantly changing values.

What changes most in this process are the competencies that the organization values in its employees: the skills that people are expected to possess in order to succeed in the organization. Competencies, like values, are situational—that is, they flex constantly in order to meet the changing needs of the organization. Values and competencies, in fact, are closely linked. Management development focuses more on people's competencies than on past job performance. An employee's value is judged more by competency than by history. Most people, however, focus more on their job performance than on the competencies that upper management values. This is not to say that job performance is no longer important. Job performance gets you noticed. But it is competencies that get you promoted!

Obviously it's important to understand what competencies are currently of value to your organization—and then strive to develop these skills (see Exercise 15). Competency-based performance management systems have become very popular in recent years. In these systems, the desired competencies are clearly identified. There may be programs and training available for employees to develop these skills. Sometimes the desired competencies for each job are listed as well so that everyone understands what skills are needed to aspire to that position. As the value of the job changes, so too should the competencies. For example, what competencies would someone need in an organization undergoing significant change? These attributes might include flexibility, resourcefulness, creativity, perseverance, and openness.

Different Sides of Change

We all have our own unique perceptions—the way we see the world. One person can see one thing and someone else can see an entirely different image. Our perceptions are first formed in childhood and become strengthened over the years. Thus changing your perceptions—the lens through which you view yourself and your role in the organization—is never an easy task.

How you perceive change is a unique experience. How you're affected personally, of course, will have a strong influence on your perception of the change. If the impact is positive, you're likely to perceive the change as a good thing. But the power of perceptions goes even further. Different perceptions can cause people to miss important aspects of change that can be critical to dealing with change successfully. It all depends on what side of it you're looking at.

The change box in Figure 11 (page 92) illustrates some of the various ways in which you might perceive change. Look at side A of the change box. What do you see? Which side of the change box is it? Do you see side A as the top of the box, the inside back, or the outside back? If you turned this box over, where would side A appear?

Often we see only one side of an issue. What if you looked at change from a different perspective? What if you looked at the B side of change instead? Again, would everyone look at this box and see the same thing? One person might look at change and see the C side, another the D side. The change box illustrates that change can be

NEW SKILLS
FOR CHANGING TIMES

1. Even if your organization doesn't have a formalized system, it's important to recognize the significance of competencies—particularly during times of change. What skills are currently important in your organization?

....

....

....

....

....

2. Do you think you're considered to possess these key competencies? Or do you need to develop them? List the competencies that would be considered your strengths:

....

....

....

....

....

3. Now list the competencies you'll need to develop to meet the changing demands of your job and the organization:

....

....

....

....

....

viewed from different perspectives. And there are many dimensions of change that go unnoticed. Ultimately it depends on how you view change. You can perceive it from just one side or you can look at it from a multidimensional perspective to fully understand its meaning.

How would you open this box to see its contents? Sometimes it's important which side of the box you open. If you always approach change the same way (open the change box from the same side), you'll always see change from the same perspective. But what if you opened the change box from a different side—say side D instead? Would the contents appear to be different? Work through Exercise 16 to explore your perspective of change.

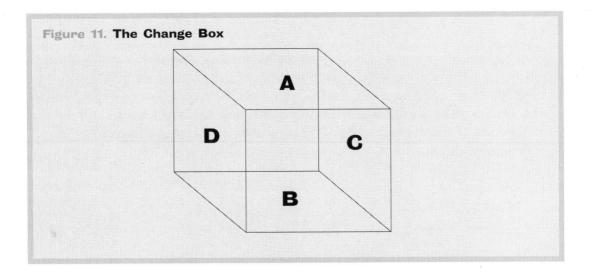

Figure 11. The Change Box

Unexpected Consequences

Sometimes you can open a box and be completely surprised by its contents. You never know what you might discover when you open that change box. Change brings disappointments as well as surprises. But the most interesting thing about change is that you never really know what to expect. Sometimes change takes you in the direction you want to go and sometimes the other way. Whatever the case, you need to hold on because it's probably going to be an exciting ride.

This is where you really need to begin thinking about how you can make change work for you. The best thing about change is that it creates

LOOKING AT YOUR CHANGE BOX

How can you apply the principles of the change box to your working environment? How can you look at change from a different perspective? What's the *other* side of change for you?

1. What's your usual perspective of change? Which side of the change box do *you* tend to see?

....

....

....

....

2. What do you think would happen if you viewed change from an entirely different perspective? What effect would this have on your current view of change in your workplace and life?

....

....

....

....

new opportunities every time it appears. It's up to you to take advantage of them. When life gives you lemons, make lemonade. In other words, find ways in which change can work to your advantage. Maybe you need to look at a different side of change. Sometimes you need to create your own opportunities. At other times opportunity bangs on your door and asks if you're ready. But you have to get up off the sofa to let it in! You need to be in a constant state of readiness. If it takes you too long to get yourself mentally, emotionally, or physically ready for an opportunity, it may just pass you by. Change is impatient.

It gives you only a narrow window of opportunity to avail yourself of its benefits. It seldom gives you a second chance. Before you know it, it's knocking on someone else's door who may be better prepared to accept its challenges and rewards. The Latin phrase is *carpe diem:* Seize the day.

But you can't expect to seize an opportunity if you're not prepared for its arrival. Don't allow yourself to be caught completely off guard. Your radar screen should prevent that from happening. If it doesn't, then you should be paying more attention to blips on the screen that hint what the next change might be (see Exercise 17.) One thing is always certain: Change will come before you're ready for it. It's usually ahead of its time. Often it disguises itself as something that isn't needed at the time. Because it isn't yet absolutely necessary, it will meet with a certain amount of resistance from those who are quite pleased with the way things are going. All of these elements of change cause it to create unexpected consequences.

IS THERE A HURRICANE ON YOUR HORIZON?

——

Even when you do get some warning that change is coming, there still will be unanswered questions. Sometimes change is like a hurricane headed for a coastal community. Even when it's spotted on radar, it still can move in unpredictable ways. We can predict with some certainty that it's coming, but not where it will hit and with what intensity. It's like trying to decide which direction a spinning top will move on a linoleum floor. The tiniest crack or speck can cause it to spin in an entirely different direction.

1. If change is a hurricane, what name would you give the next one you see on your early warning radar screen?

....

2. Where do you think this one will hit?

....

....

....

....

3. What unexpected directions could this change take?

....

....

....

....

....

4. What unexpected consequences might this change create?

....

....

....

....

5. How might these unexpected consequences present opportunities for you?

....

....

....

....

6. How could you take advantage of these opportunities to make change work for you?

....

....

....

....

....

....

7. Where is the eye of this storm? In other words, what's the center of the forces created by change in your organization?

....

....

....

....

Chapter 7

Learning the Politics of Change

—

If you're lucky, with change will come directions from the initiators concerning the new rules of the game. The best change initiatives provide this kind of communication to every change target in the organization. If this information is presented to you, listen carefully. It will give you valuable insights into what's now of most importance to the organization. But playing by the rules is sometimes not enough. In most organizations, a lot of other factors will have an impact on change and its effects on people. This is often referred to as the politics of change.

When you hear the term *politics*, what images come to mind? You may be reminded of the Republican and Democratic national conventions with all their pageantry held every four years to nominate their candidate for president. You may be thinking of the primaries leading up to this nomination and all the promises and speeches that everyone must endure. Or you may focus on the political process itself with its power struggles and influence peddling. Recent events may also conjure images of scandals and lies. Whatever comes to mind when you hear this term, it's a pretty sure bet you were not picturing a system that you'd consider fair and equitable. There are just so many external factors that go into politics—factors that may seem ugly but apparently are necessary for the process to function.

Ultimately the politics of organizational change may come down to a simple axiom: "It's not what you know but who you know." If you don't impress the right people, your career may not take you where you really want to go. For many people, this is not happy news. They may denounce the political process in their organization and deny any intent to participate in it. But you can't deny that it exists. Politics is part of every corporate decision and every change.

Like it or not, understanding the politics of change will help you deal more effectively with change. If you're one of those who hates anything that even hints of politics at work, you need to pay particularly close attention to this chapter. Not only will it help you understand this political process, but it will show you how you can make it work for you without compromising your ideals.

Political Campaigns

An essential part of the political process is the campaign. Campaigning means letting others know what you want to do and how you intend to do it. It involves gaining their confidence and support to help you get where you want to go. In a political campaign, candidates try to convince the voters that they can serve their needs best and deserve their support. Whether at work or in public office, politics means trying to satisfy the goals of as many people involved in the process as possible. This is no easy task. Think of all the different special interest groups with divergent and sometimes conflicting objectives. Pleasing one group without alienating another is a skill that politicians have tried to master since the first public official took the oath. Few have learned how to achieve this balance; many miscalculate whose needs are most important. Sadly it's often their own needs that assume primary importance rather than those of the people who put them in office.

There are important lessons to be learned from the political process when it comes to dealing with organizational change. The politics of change need not be negative. Politics can help you as well. Even politicians keep their campaign promises from time to time and provide the services they were elected to deliver. Organizational change can deliver a better system for you to work in—a system that will help you achieve your goals for the future. But you have to understand at least some of the politics both aboveboard and behind the scenes (but still very much part of the process). Appreciating these lessons can help you understand how the politics of organizational change affects *you*. Now let's take a look at these lessons.

Know Who You're *Really* Working For

Knowing who you *really* work for is not always easy to understand. Wouldn't this be your immediate supervisor? That may be who you report to officially on the new organizational chart, but the reality of the situation may be entirely different. The real question is this: Who is really in charge? Who has the real influence? Who needs to sign off on important matters?

Understanding who's really in control is extremely important during times of change. In transition periods where responsibilities are being transferred from one person to another, lines of authority can get blurred. The best way to understand who's really in charge of you is to follow the decision trail. This is the path a decision must follow in order for something to happen. Of course, different decisions need to be made at different levels in an organization. In your case, the decisions to follow are the routine approvals you need in order to function in the organization. Follow the decision trail till you reach the highest level to which you must go to get the answers you need to perform your job. Knowing who makes these decisions will give you valuable insights into the way your organization will function for the immediate future.

Understand the Problems of the Past

The first thing a good politician does is look at the problems that people have had in the past—and then promise to make things better in the future. This is what organizational change is all about: a campaign promise made by someone on some level of the organization. Often the goal is for the new system to differ from the old one as much as possible. Sometimes it is only to tweak what already exists—to adjust it and make it work more efficiently. Again, not understanding the intent of the change is like dancing to the wrong tune. If you go around proposing that extensive spending is the right direction for the organization during an era of stringent cost cutting, for example, your ideas will not be very well received.

Find New Ways to Solve Problems

Try using the new system to solve problems. Everyone will be eager to test the changes to see how they handle the problems they were designed to address. The more you can solve problems utilizing the changes, the happier everyone will be with the results you achieve. By doing this, you validate the necessity for the changes (and those who stuck their necks out to make the changes happen will be exceptionally pleased).

Pay Attention to the Reactions of Others

Just as politicians watch the polls to follow the public's reaction to their proposals, the initiators and implementors in an organization must do the same. They need to understand how people are reacting to the changes. Some change by its very nature is going to elicit negative response. Not many of the change targets will welcome a corporate downsizing that directly affects them. You can gain important insights simply by checking the "public opinion" in your organization and trying to gauge the possible consequences of this response.

Remember That Support Can Shift

People's support of change can disappear with little notice. If there's even the slightest variation in the plan or something doesn't come to fruition, people's support can collapse like a house of cards. This is a particular problem for the change initiators. When they explain how the change will take place, they presume that the positive reactions they hear will continue throughout the process. Things change, however, and so do people's reactions. But the initiators may no longer be listening. They may already be thinking about the next change they need to initiate. They may assume that everything will remain as they left it. Before too long, however, they may find themselves out of alignment with the rest of the organization. They're still reading yesterday's newspaper while everyone else has this morning's edition.

Don't Forget—People Have Long Memories

Implied or not, a promise is a promise. In other words, people remember anything that even sounds like a promise for a long time—even forever. Have you ever heard someone talk about a company's promise to their parents, grandparents, or other relatives? Often they can tell you in great detail how this convenant was broken. These stories are even passed down through the generations as part of a family's heritage. Obviously promises are powerful because people believe them. If you promise that something is going to be better because of a change, you'd better make good on your word. If you don't, the promise will become a living legacy of your credibility and trustworthiness.

How seriously do people take promises about organizational change? It depends on their experience with the initiators' ability to come through with the goods. If the initiators have a good track record, chances are that people will feel confident about the change and support it. If not, they'll listen politely but in their hearts they'll be very skeptical that anything promised will ever be delivered. But generally people want to believe what they're hearing. There has to be *some* reason for all the hardship and sacrifice they must go through as a result of the changes.

Politicians are full of promises. Usually it's easy to see if these promises have any likelihood of being fulfilled. If they're empty, you'll know how seriously to take them. If you believe they'll be fulfilled, then that's the direction you should be aligning yourself for the future.

Don't Discount the Power of Image

To the person experiencing it, perception is reality. What is real or the truth may sometimes take a backseat to how people perceive it. This may explain why certain politicians get reelected term after term despite miserable legislative records. The political landscape is littered with examples of image taking precedence over qualifications. Think about the Nixon/Kennedy debates that so heavily influenced the outcome of the 1960 presidential election. Or the Clinton/Dole presidential race in 1996. What influence did image have on these elections? Who were the most qualified candidates for the job and who had a better image? In these cases, image changed the course of history. What if Vice President Nixon had been elected president in the 1960 election? Or if Senator Dole had defeated President Clinton in 1996? Although we'll never know the answers to these questions, there's no doubt that image plays a tremendous role in the outcome of presidential elections and many other important facets of our lives.

Never discount the importance of image. It can be a powerful influence on organizational change. It can push logic and reason aside in the process. Image can turn your hundred-page business proposal into confetti faster than any other single influence. Ultimately image is king. It rules the way investors look at the company's stock. It dictates how financial analysts bestow their blessings or curses on organizations with their fateful buy or sell recommendations. It determines how customers feel about doing business with the company. It even determines how employees feel about working for the organization.

Know That What Goes Around Comes Around

Everything seems to have a way of finding its proper place in life. Often things are fairer than we believe them to be. Politicians who break the law or abuse their elected office, for example, do pay the price for their behavior. Illegal acts do result in punishment. Presidents are forced out of office, congressmen are censured and fined, and those whose job it is to send criminals to jail are sent there themselves if they break the law.

The bottom line is this: You can't cheat organizational change. Being anything less than straightforward and honest will only come back to haunt you later on. Sometimes these efforts to conceal information ultimately cause more problems down the road. Keeping certain information confidential will be understood by those who don't have a need to know it. But blocking off legitimate communications to the targets of change will only make people suspicious. If the organization has a history of guarded communication with its employees, this situation isn't likely to improve during times of change. And this will not help the change go more smoothly.

Thinking Politically

It is not always easy to think politically. And, as noted, some people have a strong aversion to thinking this way. Certainly politics brings a lot of negative images and baggage along for the ride. Regardless of how you feel about this subject, it's important to think strategically (referring to the entire organization) in the decisions you make. To do otherwise is to ignore factors that have a great impact on the success of your efforts. It's like precisely following every step in the process but one. Unfortunately, that one missed step can negate all the others. To leave out this step is to invite frustration and even failure. It just takes too much effort to do everything right and then have it all taken away because you didn't account for the politics. Even though you may not control these aspects of organizational change, you can still exert your influence.

The main thing to understand about organizational politics during times of change is where all the players have landed. Pay attention to who came out on top and who didn't fare so well. Whose court is the game being played on now? Where are you playing? Do you even know what the game is? Are you trying to throw the football to a player who's no longer in the starting lineup or even on the team? (For a look at politics and power in your organization, see Exercise 18 on pages 103 through 105.)

What if you do find you're playing in the wrong game? Let's say the changes have left you in an aspect of the business that is no longer

POLITICS AND POWER

Think of yourself as a politician and the people in your organization as the voting public. The media in this case is what's being said about you. It's the organization's collective image of you.

1. Whose political party is presently in power in your organization?

....

....

2. What effect have recent changes had on this power structure?

....

....

....

....

3. Are you a "card-carrying" member of the party in charge? If not, should you sign up?

....

....

....

....

4. What is this party's position on the big issues facing your organization?

....

....

....

....

5. Do you support the incumbent party in the organization? Explain.

....

....

....

....

6. In light of all these political considerations, what are your chances of attaining the position you wish to occupy some day?

....

....

....

....

7. Who do you think you'd be competing against for this job?

....

8. What campaign issues might determine the final results?

....

....

....

....

9. What mudslinging might occur during this competition?

....

....

....

....

10. What effect would this have on the organization's collective image of you?

....

....

....

....

where the action is. In this case it's important that you don't get forgotten by the rest of the organization rushing along in the fast lane while you're in the slow-speed zone. Your best resources are your contacts throughout the organization. You need to connect and reconnect with these people. Find out how you can contribute from your new position. Regardless of what team you ended up on, you still need to be a team player. This is the best image you can create for yourself.

Remember that ultimately you will be judged not by how upset you were by the changes, but by how much you contributed to their implementation. Don't invest all your energy in making everyone understand how unhappy you are with the way things turned out. Instead of telling everyone how mad you are that you didn't get what you wanted and sulking away to your office, invest your energy in positive directions. Maybe Richard Nixon could get away with saying to the media after losing the 1962 California governor's race, "You won't have Nixon to kick around anymore," and still be elected president a few years later. But statements like this, even under the most stressful and emotional circumstances, are still long remembered and often are held against the person one way or another.

Image Making

You need to think about the image you project to the rest of the organization. Are you satisfied with how others see you? Advertising and public relations firms are constantly remaking people's images. Products are constantly being repackaged in different ways to change how people think about them. So why can't you change your image in the organization?

This image needs to go beyond the collective impression of you created for purposes of management development. This is a more universal image of you in the corporation. It's what everyone thinks about you, not just the decision makers. The good news is that this image is more easily changed than the collective impression formed by the decision makers. Your coworkers have more frequent contact with you and consequently get to know you better than the decision makers. Their image of you is often the more accurate of the two impressions because it's based on current experience and reality. The flip side is that because it's so pliable it can also change abruptly. All this is part of the game of image making, an endeavor you should view as an investment in your future.

Image problems are sometimes the result of misinformation. The better others know you, the more accurate their image of you will be. Politicians are keenly aware of this fact. They know they must get out in public and press the flesh. They rally people together so they can meet and greet as many voters as possible. They are constantly working the crowds and shaking hands and kissing babies. Politicians understand that media images are one-dimensional. The voting public needs a more personal introduction. So politicians migrate to town halls and public squares in an effort to ingratiate themselves to the voters. Their objective is to create a personal relationship on some level with each potential voter.

The next best thing is getting a good sound bite on the evening news (see Exercise 19). A sound bite is a brief highlight of the candidate's most newsworthy message of the day. Accompanying this sound bite will be images of the candidate being warmly greeted by crowds of adoring supporters. Sometimes a public figure's image is created by one defining moment—a moment that stays with him or her for the rest of his or her career. Think of Senator Ted Kennedy's defining moment that occurred on July 18, 1969, while taking a young woman home from a party in a place called Chappaquiddick. But defining moments don't always have to be negative. Think about sports figures. What defining moment comes to mind when you think about Mark McGwire of the St. Louis Cardinals during the 1998 baseball season? The answer has to be the moment when he broke Roger Maris's long-standing home run record established in 1961.

Exercise 19

YOUR SOUND BITE

Your collective image in the organization often resembles those sound bites on the evening news about the front-runner for a political office. The general public usually forms its collective opinion about candidates based more on these fleeting but powerful images than on what they really represent.

1. Imagine that the evening news is going to air a sound bite about you tonight. What would you want this sound bite to be? Write your thirty-second sound bite as it might appear on the local news this evening:

....

....

....

....

....

....

....

....

....

Once again, your relationships in the organization are crucial. One way to begin changing your image is to build on your working relationships with others throughout the organization. Get to know as many different people as possible. Build new connections. Find new and different contacts throughout the organization. Establish new sources of information and develop them into a network. Remember, you need to give to receive. Don't expect relationships always to be one-way. You've got to nourish them. You need to network externally as well as internally. Outsiders not only are good sources of information but also

2. How well does this sound bite represent what you are all about as a candidate for the position you hope to hold someday?

....

....

....

....

....

....

....

....

....

3. How can you bring this sound bite into alignment with your personal and professional goals in the future?

....

....

....

....

....

....

....

....

....

can provide valuable feedback. Sometimes they have a better perspective on what's really going on in your organization because they're not part of its political process. They have no vested interest other than their professional relationship with you: no axes to grind, nothing to lose by your success.

Hitting the Campaign Trail

Where would the campaign trail lead you? If you were campaigning for the job you desire, what message would you send the rest of the organization? Just as with politicians, people need to know your vision for the future. Recognition is a key element in a political candidate's success. People are not very likely to vote for a candidate they know nothing about. This highlights the importance of visibility in a situation where other people's opinions matter a lot. Thus it's important for you to seek, not avoid, visibility—particularly visibility in the view of the change initiators in your organization. Either figuratively or literally, you need to get your name in the paper. Find ways to gain recognition for what you've accomplished. Use the electronic tools available today such as e-mail and voice mailboxes to ensure that the right people know what you're doing. Look for other ways to publicize your accomplishments such as trade journals or professional affiliations.

Think of any new assignment as an opportunity to gain greater recognition. These are the things that shape people's image of you throughout the organization. Few things make such an impression as a distinguished war record. You need to make known your own "war record" filled with stories of hard-fought battles you've been engaged in during your career. This is not the time to be modest. Let others know what you have accomplished or are capable of achieving. Take advantage of every opportunity to let others know what you can do.

Political candidates always seem to have standard stump speeches they give over and over on the campaign trail. Although you may hear variations of these themes tailored for a particular audience, the message is essentially the same. The candidates spend a lot of time with political strategists crafting these speeches to ensure that they hit all the right points and gain them as many votes as possible on their campaign trail. Although you may never be given the opportunity to address massive crowds anxiously awaiting your message, you will have chances to make a statement about your contributions to the organization. These opportunities, however, usually present themselves without advance notice. They may even occur at the most unexpected times. For most people in an organization, exposure to the top executives is infrequent and brief: a fleeting moment in an elevator, passing in the hallway, or even in the lavatory while washing your hands. So you must be prepared to present your campaign stump speech quickly and concisely at any time and place. But unlike the presidential candidate about to address his party's national convention with everyone waiting patiently, you have only a few moments at best to be heard. Don't squander them on small talk (see Exercise 20).

The Gatekeeper Effect

A gatekeeper is someone in the organization who has the power to make a significant impact on your career. He or she can, in a very real sense, open or close the door to your future advancement in the organization.

Typically, but not necessarily, gatekeepers are supervisors. They may be in management positions several levels above you or even in lateral positions. Whatever they are, they play a critically important role in your future—particularly during periods of organizational change. Your gatekeeper controls what the outside world hears and thinks about you. In many ways, your gatekeeper is like your public relations manager or press agent.

Unfortunately, many people don't take good care of their gatekeeper. They may not appreciate just how important their gatekeeper is to their career. You need to help your gatekeeper open doors for you. Even gatekeepers have others they must persuade to let you pass through. They have a tough job, so try to make it easier for them (see Exercise 21 on pages 112 and 113).

Remember that gates can swing both ways. This means that a gatekeeper can just as quickly slam the gate closed as open it for you. Sometimes it takes only one person in a gatekeeper role to make or break your career. What effect did Frank Hawkins have on Mary Cramer's career in Chapter 5? In his gatekeeper role Hawkins did everything in his power to block Mary's progress through her career gate at ZenTec.

One thing you don't want is for your gatekeeper to give you a bad name. This can be particularly damaging to the organization's collective

YOUR ELEVATOR SPEECH

———

Picture this scene: You've just walked into an elevator and realize you're alone with the CEO of your organization. To your surprise, the CEO says hello to you by name. She's also remarkably aware of your current assignment and asks you a question that demonstrates a general understanding of what you're trying to achieve. This is your big opportunity to make a favorable impression. Remember, you have to complete your entire presentation before the elevator doors open and the executive rushes off to her next meeting. What will you say?

....

....

....

....

....

....

....

....

....

....

....

....

....

....

....

....

HELPING YOUR GATEKEEPER HELP YOU

It doesn't matter if a gate is made of the strongest metal or is simply a mental barrier. Gates can still prevent you from moving forward in your life.

1. Who are the gatekeepers in your career?

....

....

....

....

....

2. What might be locking the gates to your future career development?

....

....

....

....

....

3. How can you make this role easier for your gatekeeper?

....

....

....

....

....

4. What are some of the gates you must pass through on your career path?

....

....

....

....

....

5. Where might some of these career gates lead in the future?

....

....

....

....

....

impression of you. Remember, these are the impressions that can be the hardest to change. Even worse, you may not always know who your gatekeepers are or what their personal impressions of you are. They may indeed be those trolls on your career bridges that are part of your worst nightmares. As in the case of Mary Cramer, you may not even know if they're friend or foe.

Mentors and Tormentors

We've all had gatekeepers who were either mentors or tormentors in our lives. Mentors are our supporters; tormentors are our detractors. Most people experience a "wicked witch" of one sort or another in their career. Just like the one who tormented Dorothy in the classic movie *The Wizard of Oz*, we've all encountered someone who seems to be out to get us. How real this may be is debatable, but the feeling is always the same. No matter what we do, we're afraid our tormentor will still find something to criticize.

Change can bring the unexpected. Sometimes it may even drop a house on top of your wicked witch. But be careful before you begin your celebrations. Just as in the story, there may be another one who's meaner than the first! You're not in Kansas anymore. The organization has changed, and you can never go back to the old one. Maybe you need to get along better with the new witch than you did with the old one. You may find that the witch is not really so unreasonable after all.

If you've made an enemy of a powerful witch, you'd better find out why. This is where having a mentor can be invaluable. Sometimes the best mentors in our lives are the ones we choose for ourselves, not those who are assigned to us. Your mentor's success can help you in many ways. You may even be perceived more positively if you have the right mentor. This is the opposite of the guilt by association described in Chapter 5. Have you ever heard of the principle of "drafting" in race car driving? Drafting is an aerodynamic effect that enables the others behind the leader to move forward with less effort as a result of the lead car's pull. The faster the leader moves, the more others behind are helped. Often a mentor's success brings good things in its trail for the protégé as well.

Ask your mentor how you can change other people's impression of you. Even though these perceptions may be based on limited information, perception is reality to these people. Your goal is to do whatever you can to change their perceptions about you. The following chapters will teach you how this can be done.

Chapter 8

Climbing the Career Ladder

Change can put you in unusual situations. It can also interrupt your career's upward progress and prevent you from reaching your goals. Although it may not always seem that you're in control of your own destiny, it's still up to you to climb your own ladder of success. But before you start any big initiatives to take charge of your career following organizational change, it might be best to let the dust settle. This will give the new organization a chance to emerge and develop. If your career barely survived these changes, remember that things could be worse. Even though you may not be happy about where you ended up, at least you're still on the organization's reporting chart.

Consider this most recent reorganization a wake-up call. If you don't do something, you may not be so fortunate next time. The first step is to take responsibility for your career. If you think there's someone in your organization working out the details of a master plan for your career, you're going to be disappointed. Ultimately you have to take charge of your own career. No one else can do this job for you. After all, it's you who have the greatest vested interest here.

If you're feeling that organizational change has damaged your career, you need to understand that the change initiators probably didn't bear you any ill will personally. They were just trying to design a new organizational structure to react to a change event. Sometimes organizational change is like trying to fit tiny pieces into a giant jigsaw puzzle. If pieces don't fit, sometimes they get forced into positions where they don't really belong. But they're all still part of the puzzle. The initiators know that to leave out any of these pieces will create serious gaps in the new organization.

Often things don't become clear until you learn something new. As pieces of the puzzle begin to fit together, other bits of information suddenly have new meaning. Fitting in additional pieces of a jigsaw puzzle allows you to see where others should be placed. Where *you* fit into the new organization's design may not be clear. But by this time the change initiators may be focused on the next change event coming their way. This is why it's essential for you to take charge of where your career is headed. You're the only one who will be thinking about your own individual needs. This doesn't mean you shouldn't be working toward the organization's goals as well. It's just that you're the one who must make sure your personal goals stay aligned with those of the organization.

Ten Rungs on Your Career Ladder

Figure 12 depicts ten rungs on your career ladder that can make change work for you rather than against you. Be careful not to get stalled on any single rung that might prevent you from reaching your ultimate career goals.

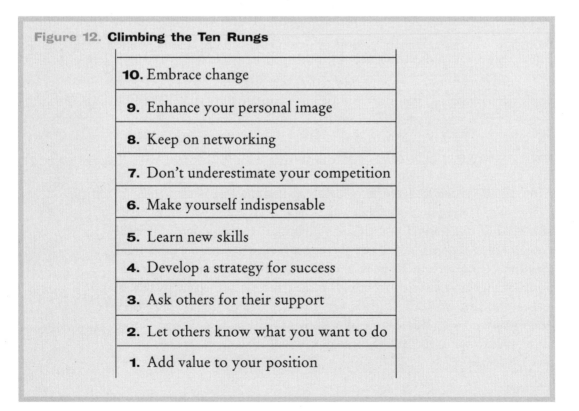

Figure 12. Climbing the Ten Rungs

10. Embrace change

9. Enhance your personal image

8. Keep on networking

7. Don't underestimate your competition

6. Make yourself indispensable

5. Learn new skills

4. Develop a strategy for success

3. Ask others for their support

2. Let others know what you want to do

1. Add value to your position

Rung 1: Add Value to Your Position

Your job, like your home, is your castle. If you don't see value in it, why should anyone else in the organization perceive it this way? You need to recognize the value of your new position. After all, there must have been some reason why the change initiators put this position in their organizational design. To devalue your job would be a slap in their faces. Although you may be thinking this is not such a bad idea, you need to get over these feelings. Give that wastepaper basket another kick across your office if you need to and start thinking about how you can add value to your new position.

Think about how much importance a job takes on once it gets the attention of top management. Something that was once relegated to the lower depths of the organization suddenly takes on new meaning. Take, for example, the issue of quality. Remember how most people in the organization viewed quality a decade ago before it was popularized by such management gurus as W. Edwards Deming, Philip Crosby, and others? Most likely quality was viewed as the responsibility of the Quality Assurance Department and nobody else in the organization. Today the new emphasis on the quality process has changed that old perception forever. Quality now is an essential area of focus on all levels of the organization and fundamental to remaining successful in today's ever-competitive markets. The quality process didn't introduce anything new. All it really did was elevate its primary importance in the eyes of the organization.

What brought about this new perception was a change event—in this case, a rapid decline and subsequent crisis in the quality of the goods and services businesses were producing. For American businesses, foreign competition (particularly from Japan) was taking away an alarming percentage of their market share. This provided the wake-up call. The question you should be asking is this: What's *your* wake-up call to the rest of the organization concerning the value of your position? How can you sound the alarm that the organization should be paying more attention to your new role? The real challenge is doing this without sounding like an alarmist going around crying "My career is falling, my career is falling!"

No matter how insignificant your assignment may feel, you should view your responsibilities as essential to the business's success. Just like the unsung heroes of sports who toil without celebrity, you may need to provide services that allow the superstars to succeed. Usually those in support roles get little notice—unless they fail to fulfill their duties. The same will be true for your assignment. It may get little attention—unless you fail to perform your tasks properly. Then all hell will break loose and you'll get more attention than you ever wanted.

An attitude of just getting by with the basic requirements is likely to sentence you to a very long stay in that dead-end job. Performing at that level can get you stalled on the first rung of your career ladder. Meeting the minimal requirements will probably keep you out of trouble, but it will also keep you from being noticed by anyone in a decision-making position. You need to get out of the cellar. The best way to do this is by proving that you can do more than what you're presently being asked to do. But remember, if you belittle your assignment, you also belittle your accomplishments in that role. This can become a vicious circle. Regardless of how you may feel about where you're assigned, you need to approach your job as if it were the keystone of the organization. Think of ways to get your position's name known and attention will follow.

Rung 2: Let Others Know What You Want to Do

There's a distinction between complaining about how badly you've been treated and letting others know what you plan to do about your future. People grow tired of hearing someone else bellyache all the time. We all have our crosses to bear, particularly during times of organizational change. Few emerge from the experience unscathed. Others have their own problems to worry about now.

But building on the first rung of the ladder—adding value to your position—can help you be heard. The better you perform your present job, the more interested others will be in hearing what you want to do in the future—particularly the change initiators. They're constantly on a scouting mission looking for talented people to fill future positions they'll create in response to the next change event. The more you distinguish yourself in your current role, the more likely it is that someone will ask you about your next assignment.

The greatest risk in your current assignment is that you may become stereotyped in this role. It's like an actress who can never shed a defining role she played earlier in her career. No matter what part she's in, the audience still perceives her as that former character. It's a public image that just won't go away. Sometimes it's best to stop fighting this image and try to build on it instead. The actress could begin to take similar roles that expand the dimensions of this character yet remain consistent with the audience's image of her. Similarly, you may need to build on the role you are currently assigned. In which directions could you progress? What are the requirements for moving up to the next rung of this career ladder?

Even if you're not interested in this career path, you still need to perform as if you were. Excellent job performance is usually seen by decision makers in an organization as being transferable from one assignment to the next. Just as good actors can play just about any part, top performers can be assigned to any job and excel.

Rung 3: Ask Others for Their Support

Most people like to help others—particularly when they feel that the other person is highly deserving. This principle leads us to the next rung on the ladder: asking for help. Don't be afraid to ask others to help you reach the next level in the organization.

But first a word of caution: When asking others for help, you often have to pay some kind of price. There is no such thing as a free lunch. Those who help you may also expect something in return. Sometimes people simply want you to remember them when you get where you're going in your career. There's nothing wrong with this. Every political process is based on this type of reciprocal support. After all, everyone wants something. People support political candidates—or rising stars in organizations—with the hope of fulfilling some aspiration of their own. But beware of help that comes with too many strings attached. This kind of help may ultimately prove to be no help at all. Don't get so caught up in your desire to get ahead that you make promises that ultimately will compromise your collective image or, worse, your principles.

Remember, too, that the help you receive usually brings with it a bit of advice. Sometimes this advice can be very useful. Most of the time it's confusing and contradictory. Take such advice with a grain of salt. Although you should listen to the lessons that others have learned in their lifetimes—they're sharing what they learned as a result of pain and sacrifice—it's unlikely these stories will help you avoid the same experiences. Even so, they should serve as a history lesson. And history does have a way of repeating itself. Organizations often progress in patterns or cycles most clearly seen from a distance and learned by studying the past.

Another thing to be prepared for is unsolicited feedback about yourself. This can really catch you off guard. Getting feedback when you're not prepared for it is like having ice water splashed in your face. In fact, accepting unsolicited feedback about yourself may be one of the greatest challenges you'll face. The challenge is to use this feedback to change the way you perceive yourself. It's one thing to change your reporting relationships in an organization. It's quite another to change your attitude and behavior. This takes the most courage of all.

Rung 4: Develop a Strategy for Success

Remember the movie *Apollo 13* when three astronauts were trapped in a crippled spaceship on that ill-fated mission to the moon in 1970? In that movie the mission flight director in Houston said something very profound about the goal to bring these three men back to Earth safely. He said: "Failure is not an option."

The first step to success means not accepting failure. This means that you need to develop a strategy for success. It doesn't have to be an elaborate plan, but it does need to provide you some guidance. This plan should have short-term as well as long-range objectives. You can include timetables indicating certain milestones you hope to accomplish along the way. But don't chisel this plan in stone. Things change. Missing a milestone is not necessarily an indication of failure. It simply means you need to adjust your strategy and establish new goals and timetables. Above all, keep looking ahead with a success-oriented perspective. Regardless of what change does to your plans, you can't give up trying to reach your goals. If you do, then you will have accepted defeat. Change will have won.

Things don't have to turn out this way. Your determination and drive to succeed can be more powerful than change. The greatest ability we have is our adaptability. If one strategy doesn't work, we need to create another. Even plans we've been working toward for years may sometimes need to be adjusted. This can be disheartening, but staying with a plan that no longer works would be even worse. It's like insisting that the *Titanic* would get you to New York on that chilly April evening in 1912. It just won't get you there.

But you don't want to abandon your plans too quickly either. Sometimes it takes time for everything to fall into place and your plan to succeed. It's like playing the stock market. The investor's goal is to buy low and sell high. In a sense, change gives you similar opportunities. As things change in an organization, inevitably there are new opportunities emerging. They might even be called bargains. You might see opportunities that no one else recognizes yet. You could be getting in on the ground floor, so to speak. Later on, when the success of these opportunities is clear, everyone will want to jump on the bandwagon. But if you've already capitalized on these opportunities, you'll be a step ahead of everyone else. So try to think strategically and plan for your future success.

Rung 5: Learn New Skills

Learning new skills adds value to your services in the eyes of the organization. It's just like adding new software to a computer or improving the efficiency of a process in which the company has made an investment. Although you may not relish the thought of being compared to a machine in the eyes of the decision makers in your organization, try to see it from their perspective. They want to get the maximum return from every dollar they invest. Training and development are investments in the organization just like any other capital expenditure. The more value you add to your services by learning new skills, the better everyone will feel about your future—including you.

Becoming an expert in one particular skill used to be a highly desirable trait. In today's world, flexibility may be more practical. The skill needed most in the future will be the ability to learn a new job. Learning new skills gets you in on the ground floor and lets you take advantage of new opportunities.

Always try to be on the cutting edge of what's about to emerge. Sometimes you may bet on the wrong horse—learn about something that never catches on—but you shouldn't look at these efforts as unproductive. They can still be valuable in helping you understand what skills you need to acquire. And this becomes very important as you move up to the next rung of your career ladder.

Rung 6: Make Yourself Indispensable

You need to learn what no one else knows—at least not yet. If a new computer program has great potential for the organization, for example, learn this program. If there are new management techniques that could revolutionize your business, learn more about them now (rather than waiting for everyone else to jump on board). Read books. Go to seminars. Follow the business publications that provide information on these new concepts. If your organization is introducing a new product, become an expert on it as soon as you possibly can. Think of it as taking out an insurance policy on your career. If you've invested in learning something that's essential for the organization—something that no one else knows anything about—your chances of staying on top are greatly improved.

Even more important to the organization is what you might know that they don't want the competition to know. Things can get very delicate here. Of course, you should never violate any confidentiality agreements you may have signed or committed to either legally or ethically. But there may be other things that your organization's competition would like to hear more about. This might be a good position for you to be in when management starts making decisions about who should be part of the new organizational design and who should be sent packing. Your special knowledge may make you indispensable.

Another way to become indispensable is to persuade the organization to increase its investment in you. Organizations don't like to walk away from big investments before they've had a chance to realize a return. Whenever you see an opportunity to have the organization invest in your development, make the most of it. Tuition reimbursement programs, special schools, managerial and executive development programs—these are opportunities in which the organization makes a significant financial investment. Not only will you enhance your skills, but you'll make the organization more committed to realizing a return on its investment. This becomes a win-win situation for both you and the organization.

Rung 7: Don't Underestimate Your Competition

Underestimating your competition is a serious mistake. The sports pages of your newspaper are filled with stories of this type of misjudgment costing the favorite team a victory or even a championship. Underestimating the competition causes you to become complacent. You lose your competitive edge. Even though you may not always think of it this way, there's always competition for your job. Today you may be thinking that if anyone really wants it, they can have it! But how would you feel if suddenly you were told that there's someone else who could do your job better? Obviously you'd be very upset. You'd wonder what you had done (or not done) to cause such displeasure.

You'd also wonder who this person might be. For just a moment, put yourself in this situation. Let's say this could actually happen due to a restructuring in the organization. What reasons would the change initiators give you for these actions? Who would be moving into your job?

The answers should tell you, first of all, where you are most vulnerable. This can give you another glimpse into the organization's collective impression of you—particularly your liabilities from the organization's perspective. Second, it should tell you who your competition might be. In any case, you may have identified some liabilities you weren't aware of. And maybe there really is someone out there with his or her sights set on your job. Maybe this scenario isn't far from reality. One responsibility of management development committees is to develop succession plans. A succession plan maps out who will fill each key position in the organization in the eventuality that it becomes vacant for any reason. Thus it's very likely that the successor for your position has indeed already been named.

There's no need to get paranoid. This is not to suggest that you should start looking over your shoulder for this person to make his or her move. Even if such a person has been identified, he or she probably is not aware of being next in line for your job. The point is simply this: There's more competition for your job out there, both intside and outside your organization, than you might realize. A certain amount of competitiveness can be helpful in an organization. Too much, however, can become destructive. You need to find that right balance between the two to keep you moving ahead and constantly improving your performance. Never assume that there's no competition for your job. Underestimating the competition can be a serious mistake that gets you stalled on this rung of the ladder.

Rung 8: Keep on Networking

You shouldn't underestimate your friends and supporters either. They too can play a key role in your career and its development. This is the opposite effect of guilt by association. Sometimes *who* you know is more important than what you know. But don't despair if you didn't happen to graduate from the same college as the CEO of your organization. There are other ways of using networking to help your career.

Throughout your career you get to know many people. It's easy to lose touch with them, though, as you move on to other jobs. We all have a tendency to do this, even in our personal lives. Think about friends you haven't contacted for years. It's not only nice to get back in touch with former colleagues but also potentially valuable to your career. Networking is a great source of information about what's about to change in your organization—allowing you to be better prepared. Your networking contacts may be able to give you useful information and vice versa. Even better, they may mention your name to people who happen to be key decision makers or change initiators.

Your card file containing the names and phone numbers of acquaintances and friends may be one of the best tools you have to climb your career ladder. Keep in touch with these people. They are an important part of your past. They may be just as important to your future.

Rung 9: Enhance Your Personal Image

What image do you have of yourself? In the last chapter we talked a great deal about your *collective* image and how to improve it. Image can be personal as well. Your personal image is what you think about yourself. Much of this image is determined by the messages you send and receive about yourself. Each of these messages is like voice mail you send to yourself about you. Do you hear messages like this: "I'm going to do a *great* job on that new assignment"? Or do you hear this: "I just know I'm not going to shine in this new job"? The message you send yourself can have a significant impact on the results you achieve.

This principle of sending yourself positive messages is frequently used by sports psychologists. Their goal is to help athletes perform at their highest level in competition. They teach the basketball player to visualize making every basket before releasing the ball. They teach the ice skater to picture that triple axel perfectly as she prepares her routine. Golfers are taught to focus on swinging the club correctly rather than think about all the things they might do wrong. After winning a major tournament, a professional golfer was asked about one of the few poor shots that she had that day.

> *Interviewer:* Congratulations on a great victory today! It looked like you almost lost the lead near the end of the day. What about that second shot you hit on the seventeenth hole? That really seemed to get you in a lot of trouble for a few minutes. You found yourself about ten feet off the fairway with a lot of trees in front of you. You must have been worried. Did you think this mistake

might open the door for the others who were chasing close behind all day—particularly with only one more hole to play? What was going through your mind at that time? Were you scared?

Golfer: I'm sorry. I don't remember that shot that you're asking about.

Interviewer: Surely you must! You were trying to get to the green with a seven iron on the next-to-last hole. It almost cost you the tournament. If it weren't for the magnificent wedge shot you made over all those trees, you wouldn't have been able to save your par and go on to win the tournament.

Golfer: No, I'm sorry, but I don't recall that shot. But I do remember that wedge shot over the trees. That was a really tough shot that I'm just glad got over all those tall trees in front of me. Fortunately it landed just below the flag and gave me a good shot at sinking the putt to par the hole.

Interviewer: I just can't understand how you could forget a shot like that. It could have had disastrous consequences for you. But anyway, congratulations on winning the tournament today and making that great shot over the trees to save your victory.

Golfer: Thank you. That's one shot I'll remember for a long, long time!

The interviewer just didn't get it. The professional golfer was putting that bad shot out of her mind. Why should she dwell on that one mistake? What would that prove? The answer is nothing. It would only erode her confidence and possibly cause more bad shots. In this case, the golfer did just the opposite. Instead of thinking about the bad shots she made that day, she chose to focus on the good ones. *These* are the shots she wants to be replaying through her mind as she steps up to swing the golf club in next week's tournament. This is what will help her continue to win rather than go into a slump and lose her competitive edge.

Your personal image is not only a mental exercise. It can be physical as well. How do others see you? Do you project the physical image that's consistent with your goals? This doesn't have to be a beauty contest. Nor does it mean that you have to empty your bank account buying a new wardrobe. It refers to looking and even dressing the part you want to play in the organization. We're talking about the image you project. If you want to be perceived as a professional, then look and act like one. If you want to be perceived as an executive, then look and act like one. The way you feel about yourself will shape how others see you. Even the way you carry yourself can influence the organization's collective impression of you. If you display confidence in yourself, others will tend to perceive you that way. If you look hopeless, that is how others will feel about you. You need to believe in yourself. If you don't, no one else will.

And don't forget to clean up your room. Your image in the organization includes your office or workspace. How do you feel when you go into someone's office and find a disorganized mess? Does this give you confidence in that person? What happens when you enter an office that's well organized and neat? How do these images reflect on the person who occupies this workspace? How does it reflect on this person's self-image? How would you rather be perceived by the rest of the organization: messy or neat? How would you rather feel about yourself?

Take this quick test: If the head of your organization walked into your office right now, what impression would he or she get? If your answer is anything less than favorable, you'd better start cleaning your office right now.

Rung 10: Embrace Change

Embracing change means that you not only accept it but actually look forward to its arrival. But first you need to end your war on change. You need to begin thinking of change not as the enemy but as part of your allied forces to help you deal with the future. You really have no other choice. Change is bigger and more powerful than any other force you'll ever face. With or without your consent, it will march forward.

Think, for example, how the electronic age has changed our lives in ways that would have been unimaginable just a few years ago. Those who resist its influence lose the battle as well as the war. Few jobs have not been reshaped by the electronic revolution that's taking place in the world today. Probably this new technology has made your own job easier and more efficient. The Internet has made it possible to instantly access real-time information that used to take days and even weeks to receive. It also has enabled managers to expand their span of control to far-reaching locations via these new electronic tools.

The advances in electronic communications make it possible for you to be reached by anyone, anywhere, anytime. Whether these technological advances will ultimately improve people's lives in future generations is, of course, yet to be determined. Again it's a matter of perception. When a cell phone rings at a children's soccer game on a Saturday morning, dozens of parents check their pockets to see if their office is trying to reach them! Again, depending on your perspective, the merits of being totally accessible to your boss as you're watching your kid score a goal may be debatable.

The telephone, too, has changed our lives in many ways. Not only has it linked each of us instantly with the rest of the world, but now it has become a computer itself. Perhaps you don't think of your telephone as a computer, but that's exactly what it is. We are asked to perform any number of data entry tasks and computer applications using what we used to think of simply as the numbers on our phones. We can apply for loans, make travel plans, buy and sell stocks and bonds, and initiate many other major changes in our lives via the cordless telephone in our kitchen. Alexander Graham Bell would be flabbergasted.

Reaching an answering machine rather than a live human being has become the norm today rather than the exception. What would happen if someone absolutely refused to utilize telephone answering machines? Would he or she be able to function in our automated society? Think about all the services and information that would not be available to that person. Yet you probably know people who took this position against answering machines just a few years ago when they first appeared. How long were they able to resist the impersonalization of the answering machine? Perhaps at first they were able to hold their position and refuse to participate in this aspect of the electronic revolution. But as these machines became commonplace in our society, they really had no choice but to embrace the change. It's also likely that when you call these same people today you'll be asked to leave a message on their answering machines.

In Exercise 22 on pages 128 through 130, think about how these ten rungs might influence your climb up the career ladder. Which one gives you the most solid footing? Which ones might get you stalled?

Exercise 22
CAREER LADDER ASSESSMENT

———

This Career Ladder Assessment will help you evaluate your potential progress in the future. Is there a possible problem on a particular rung of your career ladder? If not, then climb to the next higher rung. If so, what can you do to address that problem and climb to the next rung? Start from the bottom of the ladder and climb it one rung at a time.

Rung 10: Embrace Change
Does a problem exist? If yes, what can you do to avoid getting stalled on this rung?

....

....

....

Rung 9: Enhance Your Personal Image
Does a problem exist? If not, move to the next rung. If yes, what can you do to avoid getting stalled on this rung?

....

....

....

Rung 8: Keep on Networking
Does a problem exist? If not, move to the next rung. If yes, what can you do to avoid getting stalled on this rung?

....

....

....

Rung 7: Don't Underestimate Your Competition

Does a problem exist? If not, move to the next rung. If yes, what can you do to avoid getting stalled on this rung?

....

....

....

Rung 6: Make Yourself Indispensable

Does a problem exist? If not, move to the next rung. What can you do to avoid getting stalled on this rung?

....

....

....

Rung 5: Learn New Skills

Does a problem exist? If not, move to the next rung. If yes, what can you do to avoid getting stalled on this rung?

....

....

....

Rung 4: Develop a Strategy for Success

Does a problem exist? If not, move to the next rung. If yes, what can you do to avoid getting stalled on this rung?

....

....

....

Rung 3: Ask Others for Their Support
Does a problem exist? If not, move to the next rung. If yes, what can you do to avoid getting stalled on this rung?

....

....

....

Rung 2: Let Others Know What You Want to Do
Does a problem exist? If not, move to the next rung. If yes, what can you do to avoid getting stalled on this rung?

....

....

....

Rung 1: Add Value to Your Position
Does a problem exist? If not, move to the next rung. If yes, what can you do to avoid getting stalled on this rung?

....

....

....

Ken's War with Change
We turn now to a story about a manager who had experienced many changes and was now at a career crossroads. In this case, all of these change events had been caused by acquisitions. But unlike the story of ZenTec, which was selling part of its business, Ken Jameson's company kept getting acquired. Thus Ken and his coworkers were continually having to adapt to the changes each new owner introduced.

Ken was in a difficult situation. The small company he worked for had just been bought by a larger corporation—the third time in the last ten years that the company had changed hands due to acquisition. The workers joked that if you wanted to know who you were working for that day, you needed to go out front and see who's name was now on the building. Each time, the new owner would come in full of promises about how much better the future would be under his or her leadership. And each time these promises would be broken as the new owner seemed to lose interest in the company and looked for another buyer to take it off his or her hands. It wasn't that the acquisition was a bad investment. It just required more attention and resources than anyone seemed willing to commit.

Ken's role in the company changed every time someone new took over the business. He often wondered why he had stayed so long. Maybe it was because he had begun his career with the company over twelve years ago and still felt some sense of loyalty to his coworkers— even though the corporation that originally hired them had long since gone its own way without any regard for them. There were a few others in management who had stayed on, too, despite the anxiety that accompanied each of the acquisitions. Through all of this turmoil a bond had formed between those who remained—the sort of bond that might unite survivors of a natural disaster. They all could tell stories about the problems and frustrations they had experienced during this roller coaster of company ownership over the last decade. The worst part was when the rumors began to spread that something was about to happen but no one would officially confirm or deny anything. It was this limbo period that was the most unsettling.

Ken had been put in charge of operations several times during these transition periods. Maybe this is what kept him from moving on to some other employer. He enjoyed this leadership role and was very good at it, too—a fact acknowledged by everyone who worked for him during these periods. Unfortunately, these opportunities always ended much too soon. The new owners would bring in their own management team to run the operation even though they usually didn't know the first thing about the business. Ken would again be pushed back into the shadows of the decision-making process. Although his suggestions would be heard (or tolerated), sooner or later he would hear something like: "Well, this is the way we're going to do things from now on." All he could do was watch the same mistakes being made over and over by those who hadn't learned the stern lessons he had.

The most recent change in ownership was the most frustrating. Ken had been left in charge of the business for nearly a year. Despite the uncertainty, he had made significant improvements in not only the efficiency but the profitability of the business—something no one else had been able to accomplish in recent years. For the first time in a long time, people were beginning to feel good about working there and the results they were achieving. And this time Ken was determined not to let the same thing happen that had always occurred in the past when the new management team arrived on the scene and took over. He was not going to get stalled again on this rung of his career ladder.

Once the new management team was in place, the first thing Ken did was look at his role in the organization and decide what contributions he wanted to make. To himself he pledged that he would not become just a minor player. This time he'd be a valued member of the new management team. He met with the parent company's leadership to let them know his goals and aspirations and explain how he could help make the acquisition work. He asked for their support in achieving these goals and, in turn, pledged his support to them in their new endeavor.

Ken developed a detailed plan to help them avoid the problems of the past. He was able to show the new decision makers how they could not only maintain the gains he had achieved during the last year but increase them as well. This certainly got their attention. In this plan Ken demonstrated how he could be an integral part of this success and make the greatest contribution. His overall objective was to impress on his new bosses just what a valuable asset he was to their organization. Without boasting, he also wanted to make it clear that he was better qualified than anyone else they might select to play such an important role in their new acquisition. During the last two acquisitions he had never really taken the time to make this point. There always seemed to be somebody the new owners wanted to bring in to take over Ken's role. But this time Ken was prepared and things would be different.

Ken was amazed just how receptive the new management team was to his proposal. In fact, they requested additional details and asked him to explore several other strategies his ideas had sparked. Ken had outlined several new processes he thought would give the company a competitive advantage. When he suggested that he be assigned to learning more about the technology, they agreed—and asked him to learn as much about these processes as possible.

The technology that Ken had in mind was on the cutting edge and not very well known in the industry. One of the first things he did was learn as much as he could about what *other* companies were doing along these same lines. He had a number of contacts not only within the company but outside as well. Ken had kept in touch with many of those who had decided to leave during the previous acquisitions and were working for other organizations. These contacts turned out to be an excellent source of information about this new technology and how it was being applied in other industries. Through these networking efforts, Ken was able to learn not only about this new technology but about how it could be applied in his business. In addition to doing research on his own, he also attended a number of seminars and classes about this technology. This effort required a significant commitment—of Ken's time as well as the company's resources—but it turned out to be a very worthwhile investment for everyone. Before long Ken was recognized as the most knowledgeable person in the company concerning this new technology. He had accomplished his objective: being perceived as a valuable and contributing member of the new management team rather than just a link to the company's past.

More important to Ken was the way he began to feel about himself. The previous acquisitions had taken a toll on his self-image. Each time a new owner came in and took control, he watched his role diminish. Ultimately he lost confidence in himself and his abilities. But this time he had decided to look at things differently—to get a new perspective on the situation. He decided that he was going to stay in control of his goals and ultimately his career. After all, wasn't he the same person who during the last transition had taken an unprofitable operation and turned it into a moneymaker in just one year? If he was capable of that accomplishment, surely the new owners could be convinced that he deserved a key leadership role in the future. Instead of sitting back and simply hoping that this would happen, as in the past, this time he decided to make sure it did. In fact, several of his closest friends thought he seemed much more assertive in promoting himself and his ideas. They liked what they saw, and so did Ken.

Ken had finally learned to stop fighting change and instead looked for ways to make it work. In the past he had invested so much energy in resisting the changes sweeping the organization that he had nothing left for his own growth and development. This time he decided to change the way he perceived change and align his personal goals with those of the new organization. With his energies focused in the same direction as the organization, he didn't meet the stiff resistance he had in the past. In fact, he was amazed how much easier change could be when he began looking at it in a more positive way.

Chapter 9

Forecasting Change

Wouldn't it be wonderful to have a crystal ball that could tell you what lies ahead? With this 20/20 preview of the future, every decision you ever made would be the right one.

No such device exists, of course. Not even our most powerful computers have this capacity. We have to rely on our own intuition and judgment to lead us safely into the unknown. But let's not minimize the potential of this type of insight. It may be one of the most underutilized resources we have. Often it's a question of simply tapping into this powerful innate ability. It's not a matter of magic or supernatural powers. It's a matter of strategic planning and contingency thinking. The future is not that hard to predict if you put some good thinking into the most probable scenarios and how to react. With the concepts presented in this book, you can learn how to make these important forecasts.

Of course, you can't expect to be 100 percent right in your predictions, especially when it comes to change. But your efforts to glimpse the future will at least prepare you for what's most likely to occur. This is far better than sitting back and doing nothing to prepare for the changes ahead or just hoping that you'll survive the next big one.

Just as a business develops both short-term and long-term forecasts concerning the markets and customers it serves, you need to set goals for your career. These career forecasts should be based on the same sorts of data as business forecasts: recent research, interviews, opinions, books, magazine articles, and other credible sources of information that can lead you to insights into the future. These forecasts will help prepare you for the changes you'll meet in the upcoming years. Are forecasts always right? Obviously not. But they're useful nevertheless because without them you won't know if you're heading in the right direction and poised to meet the demands of the future. Although forecasting may be little more than an educated guess, it does represent your best hope of understanding what is to come.

Just being aware that something is about to happen, however, may not prepare you for its arrival. Change can hit like a hurricane causing millions of dollars of damage and changing the lives of thousands of people. But hurricanes typically come with a fair amount of advance warning. The television networks rush in to broadcast live from those areas where the hurricane is expected to strike in just a few hours. They contrast the peaceful scene before the storm to the chaos that soon will occur. Yet despite all this advance warning, there's nothing anyone can do to prevent the destruction. Change can occur in a similar manner. Everyone may be aware of its impending arrival but powerless to do anything about it.

But no business could survive very long without at least some ability to create forecasts relating to the markets in which it competes for customers. Without these forecasts, it would have no idea what products or services it would need to provide in the future. It would be unable to react to changes in its customers' requirements, market trends, or the economy. Like weather forecasts, business forecasts must be updated constantly to reflect the most current information. A business that fails to update its forecasts will quickly find itself with stockpiles of inventory that no one wants. Mistaken forecasts cause many businesses to fail each year. "If only we'd had a crystal ball," they lament as they close their doors for the last time.

But how did their competitors manage to predict what customers would want in the future? They may not have had a crystal ball, but they had something almost as good. They had guts. They had the courage to be proactive. They were willing to invest the time and energy to use every resource that could lead them where they needed to go. They were also willing to be wrong. They understood the risks but forged ahead anyway. They were willing to look honestly at themselves and question whether they were really prepared to face the challenges ahead. If not, they were ready to do something about it. They were prepared not only to accept change but to change themselves.

The "What If?" Game

These competitors probably played some variation of the "What If?" game. This game is actually very easy to play. All you have to do is ask a series of "what if" questions about changes that might occur in the future and what you would do. The idea is to follow these "what ifs" until they take you to a point where you'd be directly affected. This will help you prepare for these eventualities—assuming, that is, that they become reality. If they don't, you are no worse off and most likely better prepared for some other change that might occur in the future.

Let's say, for example, that there's a possibility of your company merging or being bought. (Remember the case of Ken Jameson in Chapter 8?) There are any number of "what if" questions that could be asked:

- What if . . . this merger does come through?
- What if . . . this causes changes in the organization?
- What if . . . these changes involve your department?
- What if . . . these changes directly impact your job?
- What if . . . these changes affect your career?
- What if . . . this had an effect on your life?

As you play the game yourself in Exercise 23, note that the "What If" game has only a few rules:

1. Players must watch their early warning radar screen very closely for changes about to occur. When they see a blip on the screen, they should begin asking a series of "what if" questions. Players are not restricted to asking "what if" questions about blips on the radar screen, however. Anything that might represent a change in the future is allowed.
2. "What if" questions are to be shared with as many players as possible to get their views about potential outcomes.
3. The "what if" questions will differ according to the situation.
4. There are no right or wrong answers to "what if" questions at the time they are asked. Only the future will determine the accuracy of the answers.
5. There are no penalties for players who are wrong. Instead they should be rewarded for looking ahead and trying to be better prepared for the future.
6. There's no such thing as a stupid "what if" question. The only bad questions are those that were never asked—resulting in everyone being caught off guard when reality arrived.

A word of caution: At some point you'll need to stop playing "what if" and just go ahead and do it. Becoming fixated on too many "what ifs" can bring you to a standstill. Having all the data in front of you is fine. But sometimes you need to move forward despite all the signs that tell you to

PLAYING THE "WHAT IF" GAME YOURSELF

———

Now play your own home version of the "What If?" game. Answer each "what if" question and, as in the preceding example, follow the sequence of questions. If the last question doesn't lead directly to you or something you can control, continue the questioning process until it does. Begin the "What If?" game by listing a change event that will have some kind of impact on you.

Change event: ....

1. What if this change event caused . . .

....

....

....

2. As a result, what if this caused . . .

....

....

....

3. What if this resulted in . . .

....

....

....

4. What if this directly affected your life and career? What would you do?

....

....

....

hesitate. Sometimes the best decisions are the ones based on your emotions as well.

The Power of Flexibility

Not all changes begin by affecting you directly. What may look like a distant event may ultimately change your life in very significant ways. Who knows what business deal is being discussed right now in some corporate board room in a remote part of the world that could find its way into your life?

Of course, you can't do anything about a change event before you know it's actually going to happen. But by asking "what if" questions you can prepare yourself for any number of things. This can also help you develop greater *change flexibility*—that is, your ability to adapt to any kind of change. Change flexibility is a combination of your perceptions, image, skills, abilities, and, above all, attitude toward change. The more flexible about change you become, the less you need to worry when it arrives. You can even invite it into your life. The more open you are about new ways of doing things, the more you begin to exercise change flexibility. The future will belong to those who can adapt fastest to the many changes that lie ahead.

The information age is just now beginning to emerge with innovations such as the Internet and a host of other new communication tools. These are not only opening new worlds of information but causing change to accelerate at an unprecedented pace. Just keeping up is no longer enough. You need to keep *ahead* of this pace if you want to compete in tomorrow's dynamic world order. This means you've got to know what's heading your way or is just around the corner.

Beyond the question "what if?" is "what will be?" What are the changes that you'll experience in the future? What will be their effect on you, and what will you do to adapt to them? What will be the new order of things, and what will be your new role in it? These are important questions that you'll need to explore to gain some level of understanding about the future.

But before you rush off to the fortune-teller, there may be more reliable tools you can use. None of these is as good as a crystal ball, but they're the best forecasters of change you have at your disposal. Although these change forecasting tools are definitely part of the real world, they can help you explore the unknown. They're designed to help you understand what changes you may face at various times in the future and what you can do to help yourself—even when you've been yanked out of your comfort zone.

Comfort zones are the familiar patterns that make us feel secure when everything around us seems to be changing. We learn to depend on them to provide stability and consistency in our lives. Routines become habits that we learn to perform without a great deal of thought. And habits, once formed, can be very hard to break. Change is the opposite of habit. It can be like suddenly stepping into quicksand and being swallowed up without warning. Change definitely takes you out of your comfort zone. But a set of forecasting tools—called *change capsules*—can lessen the impact of being yanked out of your comfort zone by change.

Change Capsules

Remember the time capsules packed with information about current lifestyles and culture that were buried so that future generations could learn how people lived during our present time? Change capsules are designed to help you conceptualize what change may bring in the future. They can be used to help people look more strategically at their business and assess where market trends may be headed in the future. Change capsules also can help us understand how change may affect our career and ultimately our lives. They are predictions about the future that can be answered with total accuracy only after the passage of time.

Developing your own change capsules is easy. Everything you need is provided on the following pages in Exercises 24, 25, and 26. All you have to do is make copies of the change capsules to use in the future and supply an envelope for each one. To begin creating your change capsules, you will need to make certain decisions. You'll need to decide, for example, when you want to open your change capsules. Exercises 24 and 25 offer suggestions for the first two capsules, but you can choose any time period you want. It all depends on the event you're predicting. Some events may be short-term, others long-term. In either case, you'll need to specify when your change capsule should be opened again. Change capsules can become part of your strategic planning and forecasting every year. Turn them into an exercise with others at work. Have some fun with your change capsules. You might even give awards for the most accurate, the most outrageous, or the most innovative.

Change capsules are designed to help you look into the future. Although they may only be guesses, they still can offer valuable insights into the way things might change in the future. Change capsules work like this:

- Each change capsule asks you to predict what you think the future will be like on a variety of different topics.
- The first two change capsules (Exercises 24 and 25) could be used as part of a group exercise and shared with others. Change capsule 3 (Exercise 26) is to be kept personal and private. Try developing other change capsules to predict changes that could become an important part of your life in the future.
- Each change capsule has a "reveal date" indicating when the capsule is to be opened. This reveal date should appear on the envelope and be put in a tickler file to be opened at that time. On the reveal date the change capsule should be opened and evaluated for its accuracy.
- Each change capsule should be viewed as a learning opportunity. Just conceptualizing what the future might bring can be educational. History, however, is often the best teacher. As each change capsule is opened on its reveal date, you should reflect on the change events that influenced this period of time and think about how these lessons can help in the future.

CHANGE CAPSULE 1

Reveal date: ....

(One year from the date you complete the change capsule)

What major world events do you think will occur during the next year that will change the way your organization does business today?

....

....

....

....

....

....

....

....

....

....

....

....

....

....

....

....

....

....

CHANGE CAPSULE 2

—

Reveal date: ....

(Six months from the date you complete the change capsule)

1. What change events do you see coming for your organization during the next six months?

....

....

....

....

....

....

....

....

....

....

....

....

....

....

....

....

....

....

....

....

....

....

....

2. How do you think these changes will affect your department or work group and the way people perform their jobs?

....

....

....

....

....

....

....

....

....

....

3. How do you believe these changes will affect the way you perform your job?

....

....

....

....

....

....

....

....

....

....

CHANGE CAPSULE 3
(PERSONAL)

———

Reveal date: ....
(The timing is up to you)

Based on everything we've discussed in this book, think about all the possible changes you can envision for yourself between today and the date you'll
look at this change capsule again.

1. What changes do you think will occur in your professional life during this
   period?

....

....

....

....

....

....

....

....

....

....

....

....

....

....

....

....

2. What changes do you think will occur in your personal life?

....

....

....

....

....

....

....

....

....

....

....

....

3. What goals would you like to reach during this period?

....

....

....

....

....

....

....

....

....

....

....

....

....

....

4. What will you do to help yourself achieve these goals?

....

....

....

....

....

....

....

....

....

....

5. *(To be completed after this change capsule is opened.)* What were the results of your efforts to achieve the goals you established? Are you satisfied with these results?

....

....

....

....

....

....

....

....

....

....

....

....

Chapter 10

Applying Lessons in Change

The greatest lesson change teaches is pretty simple: It really isn't such a bad thing after all. Change gives you opportunities to begin again. You need to learn from the mistakes you made in the past and grow from these experiences. It would be ludicrous to continue making the same mistakes over and over without ever learning the lessons from your previous knocks. But change doesn't always have to be painful—not if you choose to welcome it for all it can teach you and all the new opportunities it can provide. It can even be refreshing. Like learning to ride a bike, the worst part of the process is the bruises you get acquiring the skills. Once you've mastered the skills, the rest of the learning can even be fun. And once you learn them, you never forget. In Exercise 27, list the top ten lessons you've learned from change.

Whether you are a change initiator, an implementor, or one of the targets, the principles presented in this book are invaluable. At different times, in one way or another, we play all of these roles in our lives. Change can be a very emotional experience. It alters people, their lives, and the sense and order of their world. Change is serious business, but you shouldn't let it become bigger than life itself. You need to keep it in its proper perspective: It's a natural principle in life and will never end. Of all the skills you can acquire during your lifetime, the ability to cope with change may be one of the most important to your future success and happiness.

Change is really nothing more than a matter of perception. It's how you *look* at change that really matters. Think of change as a second chance to get it right. Though it might seem so at the time, change is not the worst thing that could happen to you. How it affects you depends to a great extent on you. Just don't let those emotional trolls chase you off the bridges leading to your success in the future.

THE TOP TEN LESSONS

———

What are the top ten lessons you've learned from change? List them here:

1. ....
....
....

2. ....
....
....

3. ....
....
....

4. ....
....
....

5. ....
....
....

Exercise 27 (continued)

6. ....
....
....

7. ....
....
....

8. ....
....
....

9. ....
....
....

10. ....
....
....

How can these lessons help you deal more effectively with change in the future?

....

....

....

....

....

....

....

....

....

....

....

....

....

....

....

....

....

....

....

....

....

INDEX

———